BEAT PTSD

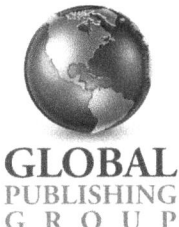

GLOBAL PUBLISHING GROUP

Global Publishing Group
Australia • New Zealand • Singapore • America • London

BEAT PTSD

How a Combat Soldier Conquered Chronic PTSD to Live a Life that Truly Matters, and How You Can Too

Kevin Lloyd-Thomas

DISCLAIMER

All the information, techniques, skills and concepts contained within this publication are of the nature of general comment only and are not in any way recommended as individual advice. The intent is to offer a variety of information to provide a wider range of choices now and in the future, recognizing that we all have widely diverse circumstances and viewpoints. Should any reader choose to make use of the information contained herein, this is their decision, and the contributors (and their companies), authors and publishers do not assume any responsibilities whatsoever under any condition or circumstances. It is recommended that the reader obtain their own independent advice. Some names and identifying details have been changed to protect the privacy of individuals.

First Edition 2018

Copyright © 2018 Kevin Lloyd-Thomas

All rights are reserved. The material contained within this book is protected by copyright law, no part may be copied, reproduced, presented, stored, communicated or transmitted in any form by any means without prior written permission.

National Library of Australia
Cataloguing-in-Publication entry:

Kevin Lloyd-Thomas
How a Combat Soldier Conquered Chronic PTSD to Live a Life that Truly Matters, and How You Can Too

1st ed.
ISBN: 9781925288162 (pbk.)

 A catalogue record for this book is available from the National Library of Australia

Published by Global Publishing Group
PO Box 517 Mt Evelyn, Victoria 3796 Australia
Email Info@GlobalPublishingGroup.com.au

For further information about orders:
Phone: +61 3 9739 4686 or Fax +61 3 8648 6871

This book is dedicated to all of those men and women who currently serve our nation, and the other free nations of the world.

It's dedicated to their families too. It's the family that bears the brunt of the aftermath of a soldier's return from a war zone.

It is dedicated to the millions of men and women, and children too, who have laid down their lives in all previous wars so that we can be free.

Freedom is not free, and never will be.

Freedom always has a price, and into eternity, there will be yet more truly unselfish and patriotic men and women who will put their lives on the line for their country, such that we remain free.

This book is dedicated to you too.

Kevin Lloyd-Thomas

ACKNOWLEDGEMENTS

Although no longer in this life, first and foremost to my Mum and Dad, Jean and David. No matter what followed, I know I was born out of love.

To my brothers and sisters, Nigel, Rosemarie, Gina and Hugh, no matter what followed for you too, you too were born out of love.

To my partner Irene, who has stuck with me through thick and thin. As I hauled myself back, and found my way out from the black abyss, it's been a hard road to hoe for her. She's had to put up with all of my ups and downs, the rollercoaster ride, and I'm so thankful for her love, support and understanding. As she put it, "You're a work in progress, and will always remain so." That's a pretty special kind of understanding.

To my former wife, Sandy Lloyd-Thomas, you gave me 32 years of wonderful marriage, and of selfless unconditional giving, no matter what. Thirty-seven years of it from the time we met. The support you've given me while writing this book has been wonderful. As I checked through my memory of many things, even though it brought up not so nice memories for you in some instances, nonetheless, you continued to give, and for that, I thank you deeply.

For those men who I served with in Vietnam, thank you for having my back for those two years. To those who have helped me to ensure I got things in order, and checked out my memory of key facts, dates times places and people, a big big thank you. It was a long time ago.

Phil Evenden, Peter "Jock" Kennedy, Ted Colmer, Laurie Tremenheere, Richard 'Barney' Bigwood, and Jim Riddle, we're mates forever. Although we may not agree on some things, it was Don Tate who was one of the major drivers in getting Jim Riddle back to Australia to get Jim a well-earned pension from DVA. Jim did three tours of Vietnam, a fierce soldier, a man's man, and we'd all have each other's back any day, and forever. Don was the machine-gunner in the section which I commanded in the 2nd D&E Platoon, and no matter what, and in front of no matter whom, I'll defend him 150% as a soldier, and a man who did his job well. He has also made a significant contribution through his two books, *The War Within*, and *Anzacs Betrayed*. They enabled me to check and to recall many facts relating to the 2nd D&E Platoon. Barney Bigwood's book, *We Were Reo's*, and Frank Walker's book, *Ghost Platoon*, helped me in the same way.

In 2012, I met a man whose wish it is to remain anonymous. He's a Vietnam veteran, and a former machine-gunner, so you know he's been right up at 'the sharp end.' You know who you are, and you'll remain anonymous past the time I pop off the planet. In 2013 he became a benefactor, and through his belief in me, and his generosity, it was he who enabled me and Irene to travel to the USA and UK, and put in place a network of amazing people. People who, already have made – and will make, even more so into the future – a massive difference in the lives of many, many veterans and their families. There's more to come as a result of this man's belief and generosity. You have my eternal gratitude.

Urban Miyares, former US Infantry Sergeant, now a great mate, has been a true inspiration. Challenged America and the Disabled Business Persons Association are testaments to what a person with severe disabilities can achieve. Joe Casal and his Vietnam Veterans newsletter has been, and will continue to be a wonderful source of information, help and support for me, and the veteran community – thanks Joe. Professor James Fallon of the University of California, and Colonel (Rtd) Jack Pryor have been great sources of knowledge and support and I look forward to working with you both into the future. The same for Delia McCabe, an inspiration. Her groundbreaking research into stress and its effect on the brain, and brain health is amazing.

There are so many other people who have given me great support and encouragement as I've travelled the path of turning my life around, being a true 'work in progress' in giving back to the community of serving men and women, veterans and their families – thank you.

To Darren Stephens, his wife Jackie, Kelly Mayne, and all the team at Global Publishing a very big thank you. You know the journey I've been on, so your support and understanding has been just wonderful.

FREE BONUS GIFT

Thank you for purchasing this book!

As a special gift, I've included some FREE bonuses for my readers.

Bonus One – How To Find Your Purpose
Bonus Two – Goal Setting Kit
Bonus Three – Health Meditation – Audio

Go to
www.BeatPostTraumaticStressDisorder.com/Bonuses

And Access Your FREE Bonuses Right Now!

CONTENTS

Introduction   1

Prologue   9

Chapter 1 – My Story   13
   Part 1 – You've Saved My Business from Liquidation:
              Thanks, But You're No Longer Wanted   14
   Part 2 – A Brutal and Violent Childhood   25
   Part 3 – My Father   33
   Part 4 – You're Not Allowed to Succeed   36
   Part 5 – Joining the Australian Regular Army   37
   Part 6 – Vietnam, Here We Come   42
   Part 7 – My Life is About to Change   51
   Part 8 – The Only War Story   59
   Part 9 – Army: Do I Stay, Or Do I Go?   63

Chapter 2 – What Was the Result?   75

Chapter 3 – Waking Up to the Problem   85

Chapter 4 – Asking for Help   91

Chapter 5 – The Rollercoaster   105

Chapter 6 – Realizing My Mistakes   115

Chapter 7 – Turning My Life Around   131

Chapter 8 – The Five-Step Life Plan   137
   Step 1 – What Do I Want To Do? What Do I Want To Be?   139
   Step 2 – Do I Stay, Or Do I Go?   147
   Step 3 – What Skills Do I Need?   157
   Step 4 – Planning and Goal Setting   162
   Step 5 – Success is Not an Accident   163

Chapter 9 – The Seven Pillars Of Success 167
    Pillar 1 – Health 174
    Pillar 2 – Happiness 189
    Pillar 3 – Wealth 193
    Pillar 4 – Purpose and Passion 197
    Pillar 5 – Spirituality 201
    Pillar 6 – Business 204
    Pillar 7 – Finance 208

Final Words 215

About the Author 219

Resources and Further Information 221

INTRODUCTION

As I've gone through this journey to where I am now, there are a few 'sayings' I've picked up along the way, quotes from various people, many I can name, others where they are anonymous, as well as my own observations.

One of the most critical I've adopted for myself, which has become one I now use in many a conversation with people from whom I am seeking information, knowledge, or their experience in a particular area of life is this:

Wherever possible, consider this – "Your mind is like a parachute… It only works when it's open."

Why has this become so critical to how I view things?

I used to be very opinionated, many things being either black or white, either one or the other, never everything in between, no 'shades of grey,' no compromise, end of story.

But as I went down the path of healing myself, becoming more knowledgeable, more aware, and more questioning, it became almost like a mantra because, in some cases, I had to, or was almost forced to question my previous beliefs, opinions, and attitudes towards certain things.

No… many, many things.

Then the further I travelled down the road to turning my life around, I realized I had to do this, or I would learn nothing. I would just repeat the same mistakes over and over and over again, but expecting a different outcome.

Pretty dumb, eh?

It made me question the prevailing wisdom in so many things, to challenge my own thinking, to ask questions in a different way, to seek more information about the latest research, then ask a question like… "If that's where the current thinking is, what about the future?" And, "How does this affect me?"

We now know far more about traumatic brain injury (TBI), *a physical injury* that occurs through being in close proximity to loud explosions, detonations and the resulting shockwaves that physically damage the brain.

Unlike a physical injury that we can see to the outer body, we do not see the damage to the brain.

We now know for a fact that a *traumatic incident physically damages the brain,* even though there is no bullet, no detonation, no shrapnel, only the traumatic incident itself.

We now know that the brain can build new neural pathways, not just for physical injuries, but for traumatic incidents as well.

Over the last ten years in particular, there have been massive advances in what we now know to be true about this through the neuroscientific research that has been carried out, and continues to expand with ever increasing vigor because of the amazing discoveries that have been made.

So that begs the question: if we now know that to be true, how much more *don't we know?*

Hence the parachute.

Introduction

This is the sort of thinking we need from the military, governments, the bureaucracy, the medical profession and the scientific community.

From my research, this will take a lot of doing, because, in many, many cases, there is still a whole lot of entrenched thinking across all these organizations and entities.

It is crucial to the current and the future wellbeing of all serving men and women, and veterans of all the conflicts of the modern era, and most particularly, for their families and loved ones, that *we open our minds to alternative therapies*, and not just cling to those that have been used in the past.

Those of us that have an open mind know that there is no such thing as 'one size fits all' anymore.

Why? Because we now have far more evidence, far more evidence-based knowledge, far more research and far more scientific proof than ever before.

So now you will know what I mean when in certain parts and topics that are covered, there is reference to 'parachute thinking,' or something like 'is this a parachute moment?'

At certain points I'll ask you to ask yourself a question, and in a couple of different ways, "Is this a 'me too' moment for you," or "Me too," or to make a statement to yourself about what you've just read… *"That's me,"* or *"That's me too."*

Why?

Because this could well be a 'watershed point' or 'watershed moment' for you. A point where you can now acknowledge to yourself that you too are heading down the same destructive path I did. One of denial, one of "There's nothing wrong with me."

A path that is full of hurt, of broken relationships with wives, children, parents, mates, colleagues and friends. A path to job loss, loss of self-belief, self-worth, self-confidence and potentially a path to self-destruction.

One of reliance on alcohol, antidepressants, legal and illegal drugs, tobacco and the like.

Then what about the anger, the nightmares, anxiety, the panic attacks, the internal rage, the explosive temper, the self-loathing, sleeplessness… and what else?

It took me a long time to realize that I was bullshitting myself.

The Kevin on the outside was not the Kevin on the inside… far from it. Is this you too?

The watershed is this: when you say yes to yourself, **"Me too,"** or **"That's me,"** or **"That's me too,"** – *you have just taken the first step of your new life.*

You can now ask for help, understanding, and support from your family and those nearest and dearest to you.

Be a team… it will work miracles for you, and I can assure you it will. There is just far too much evidence available, far too many success stories to prove that this is the path to take.

It will take courage, it will take tenacity and it will take perseverance.

Introduction

Just look at what you have faced and overcome already. But this time there is no one shooting at you, no need to be on guard, no IED's, no mortar attacks, and you are in a safe place with your family and loved ones, and surrounded by those who care for and about you.

It is very important to keep in mind that there is still, and tragically so, a lot of stigma attached to acknowledging you are having difficulty dealing with some issues and seeking help.

The greatest benefit that serving men and women, and the veterans of recent conflicts currently have, compared to their predecessors who faced WW1, WW2, Korea, and Vietnam, *is that you don't need to tell anyone except those who have a need to know.*

For currently serving men and women, don't tell anyone who doesn't need to know that you've made the decision to seek help. Why? Because they just don't need to know, and this means your colleagues, Section Commander, Platoon Commander, not anyone.

If you see the military as your chosen career, and you've said to yourself, **"Me too,"** then seek help anonymously, get back in control, and you will enhance the opportunities that come your way.

Why?

Just because *you ARE now in control*, and no matter what happens in the future, you will *always be in control.*

Through this book, you will have the tools, technique and strategies to do this.

The first book I found on PTSD and the military when researching information for this book, was *Aftershock – The Untold Story Of Surviving Peace* (Portobello Books), by British journalist and war correspondent, Matthew Green.

From Matthews book, if I could give you one piece of information, just one illustration of why you should seek help, it's this:

> "At Army headquarters near the Hampshire town of Andover, I met Captain Theresa Jackson… she showed me a selection of stories published in forces magazines based on the accounts by personnel who had successfully sought treatment for depression or PTSD. Among them was a tough Glaswegian color sergeant named Terry Lowe. A 33 year old veteran of tours in Iraq and Afghanistan, Lowe had spoken candidly about his experience of wartime trauma at a series of roadshows for younger soldiers. Nobody could accuse Lowe of being weak: he had shrugged off a suicide bombing in Iraq that killed two British soldiers and wounded more than a dozen. In an interview with Sixth Sense, the forces newspaper in Germany, he described the events in Afghanistan that caused his PTSD.
>
> I knew something was a wee bit wrong when we were caught in a horseshoe ambush and after I called in fire support to smash the compound, I found two dead civilians and five wounded that were being used as a shield by the Taliban…
>
> Shortly afterwards, Lowe trod on a pressure plate that detonated a bomb buried behind him killing two of his colleagues. The blast left him so dazed, he was momentarily convinced that he too was dead. He began to remove his helmet and body armor while bullets were still flying, and only came to his senses when others rushed to his aid. On his return home, Lowe started a classic path down the Spiral: he drank to extremes, suffered road rage and started fights. After receiving therapy from the Army, he volunteered to return to Afghanistan. Lowe proved his PTSD would not hold him back when he led his men into cover to return the fire at Taliban fighters…

Introduction

"You have got to ask yourself, if you have three of us on the ground with PTSD, and the other two aren't admitting it... who is the bigger liability?" said Lowe."

With today's technology of mobile phones and laptop computers, you can seek help anonymously, and no one needs to know except the organization or person you have contacted.

These will be organizations like the Department of Veterans Affairs (DVA), and the Veterans and Veterans Families Counselling Service (VVCS) in Australia.

The Resources Section at the back of the book lists contact details for the USA, UK, Canada and New Zealand.

PROLOGUE

How did I go from having a wonderful marriage and financial independence at 45, living a life of happiness, travelling around the world on wonderful holidays to far-off places, from planning and looking forward to being able to retire easily at 63 when my wife, Sandy turned 60, and living on an annual income well in excess of six figures a year for the rest of our lives?

To what?

I'm going to step you through my life. From a brutal childhood, to leaving school at 14 to contribute financially to my family, to drifting through life with no ambition or goals, just bitterness, and a fear and a loathing of my father, to joining the Australian Regular Army to get away from the brutality.

Two tours of Vietnam, then leaving the Army to enjoy a successful business life, and then what?

What was it that happened to me then, and later in life?

What was the result?

The 'Black Spiral' into a living hell of PTSD.

What about denial, and what happened next?

What made me reliant on that antidepressant Zoloft? A dependence on those little white pills that dragged me back up from flaying myself with self-doubt, self-pity, reinforcing my loss of self-belief, self-confidence and self-esteem?

The alcohol abuse to help me fend off the inevitable nightmares that attacked me every night, almost without letup. Four or five bottles of beer, followed by at least a bottle of wine, or even more, and every night, just to get to sleep.

Not wanting to go to bed, then the tossing and turning, waiting for the inevitable nightmares to attack me.

Almost chain-smoking 40 cigarettes or more a day, through to 20 to 25 cigars a day.

The constant anger, the frustration, the berating I gave myself on a daily basis.

What was it about this that trashed my marriage, to drive my wife away from me to the point of wanting separation, then to divorce because of all this?

After all that, because of **what I didn't know about** what Zoloft was doing, and had done to my brain, to living a life where I was totally incapable of making complex decisions.

A phase of my life that I now refer to as one where I was 'an impotent zombie.'

A phase that saw me financially wipe myself out with stupid financial decisions, not just once but twice! What the hell was I thinking?!

Living what I called a 'dual personality' life for over nine years after separation, in a twilight world of intense highs of travel, sailing, and adventure, to the deepest depths of depression and anxiety.

"The Kevin on the outside," and "The Kevin on the inside."

Prologue

Hating and despising myself so much that I planned my own suicide.

What was it that stopped me driving over that 70 meter cliff into the ocean below?

Who helped me to start on the road back from the brink of ending it all?

Then what were the steps I took to turn my life around?

What kind of a journey has that been?

What have I learned from all of this?

What happened that brought me to know that I had to write this book?

And what of the future? Where am I going, and what's my ultimate objective?

CHAPTER 1

MY STORY

CHAPTER 1 – MY STORY

Part One – You've Saved My Business from Liquidation: Thanks, But You're No Longer Wanted

The sledgehammer

My whole body was trembling so much that I could hardly control the car.

I was driving through Marsfield, a northern suburb of Sydney, and I could see the traffic lights at the next intersection change from green to orange so I knew I had to stop.

Common sense was screaming at me to pull over somewhere so I didn't have a smash and could get control of myself.

Over and over I was screaming it out loud, what the fuck did I do to deserve this?! What the fuck did I do to you or ABC Systems that you would do this to me?!

As I approached the intersection I was able to turn left and then to turn right into the car park of the El Rancho Hotel. It instantly hit me that this is where my wife Sandy and I had had our wedding reception back in June, 1971.

One day a beautiful day, this day one of torture.

What the fuck had I done to deserve this?

Chapter 1 – My Story

I found a car space, took the car out of gear and slumped across the steering wheel, my whole body shaking and trembling, exhausted, with tears running down my face. What the fuck had I done to deserve this as I smashed my fist into the steering wheel, smashed it into the door, and back into the steering wheel, again and again and again?!

Who the fuck else is bringing any money into the business? Fucking no one. Only me, you fucking asshole!

I've just saved your fucking business from fucking liquidation. Right now, everybody at ABC has a job because of me.

Why are you doing this to me, you mongrel asshole! What the fuck?

It was a round 3:30 pm in the afternoon of the 12th January 1994.

So how did this come about?

Have you ever been stabbed in the back by someone you thought was a close friend, someone you trusted and had known for 14 years? Not only backstabbed but betrayed, lied to by your work colleagues who deliberately totally distorted the truth and were believed over you, and seemingly, without question?

Little did I know that this series of events over a two-week period was to start me down the path to almost total destruction of my life.

How the sledgehammer fell

It's about 12:15 or so the afternoon on Wednesday 12th of January and Mike comes into the sales office. Mike is the owner and Managing Director of ABC Systems.

"G'day Kev, what are you working on?"

"Going over my first quarter sales forecast to make sure I'm happy with it."

Then Mike said, "Let's go to lunch," something we'd done many times together over the nine years at ABC to that point.

Over the 14 years we'd known one another, we'd also had many dinners together, not just the business dinners while at ABC. Our two wives, Sandy and Mary were close friends and we shared many social occasions together at each other's homes. We'd known the children since birth and we shared holidays together

I was a party to Mike's innermost thoughts and knew exactly the financial position of ABC.

Off we go to lunch at our favorite Chinese restaurant.

The bombshell

WHAMMO…! the bombshell I never saw coming, and had absolutely no inkling of. To the best of my recollection this is what Mike said: "This is really hard for me to tell you and I'm really sorry, but there's no longer a role for you at ABC. The company is taking a different direction, one where you don't have the computer skills needed to work in the direction I'm taking it. There'll be a bloodbath in the company as I strip it down to ensure its survival."

I was speechless, totally gob smacked by what I was hearing. I just couldn't believe what he was telling me.

My heart was pounding, my guts were churning, my mind was racing.

Chapter 1 – My Story

"What the fuck do you mean Mike…? I'm the only one in the sales team who's brought any revenue into the business in the last six months, the only one who's actually selling something. I've just saved us from being put into liquidation for fucks sake! What the fuck's happening? What the fuck are you telling me Mike? This is bullshit!"

"That's got nothing to do with where I have to take the business to protect its future," said Mike.

"But hold on Mike," I said, "What about my new role as Operations Manager that's supposed to happen in the first quarter of this year?"

"Karen Packson will have a dual role as Marketing as well as Operations Manager, and Steve Strong will have both account management and sales roles."

It was just blow after blow, like being hit in the head and the guts with a sledgehammer.

What I was being told was that the times, through my own initiative, my imagination, my creative thinking, my ability to see synergistic opportunity, and to bring it to fruition, such that the company survived multiple financial crises, it too, was worth absolutely nothing, nothing at all.

The discussion just went round and round in circles. I was out, and nothing I said would change anything, so I just got up and walked out leaving Mike at the table.

I walked across the road and back to the office, went into the sales office, grabbed my brief case and walked out. Didn't say anything to reception, just walked out with my guts in a knot, my head spinning and visibly shaking.

Day one of a three-year rollercoaster ride

That's why I was sitting in my car in the car park of the El Rancho Hotel, trembling almost uncontrollably, with tears streaming down my face, trying to get my body and my mind back under control.

Then, little did I know, nor even think of, what was about to happen to me over the next two weeks, and almost, the next three years. Why would I?

One of the worst parts for me was that on three very specific occasions I was told by former ABC colleagues that Mike quite categorically said letting me go was one of the biggest mistakes he had made.

But he never had the guts, the intestinal fortitude, the courage, but even more so, the basic human decency of saying so to me. The stuff of ethics, integrity and, most importantly, character. On the two occasions that I did bump into him by chance he told me that, although he was sorry, he had done the right thing. So who's bullshitting who?

It took over an hour, sitting in the car, in the car park of the El Rancho hotel to get back to being able to concentrate on driving home which was five or six km away. Sandy is still at work and most likely won't be home probably until about 6.30. What am I going to tell her about what happened today?

How am I going to tell her about the rollercoaster I've just been through? That morning I had left for work with a happy contented feeling. In masterminding the partnership with Computer Technologies, setting up and being a part of the Power Tools Australia sale, I'd prevented ABC from being put into liquidation by its bankers, and for the third time.

Chapter 1 – My Story

We'd just had two wonderful weeks with my family and friends over Christmas and New Year, but here I was, no longer with a job, and wondering what the future held for me?

With my brother Hugh and his family visiting from the USA, having spent Christmas and New Year with us, coming back from Melbourne on the Thursday afternoon, what was I going to tell him about what had just happened to me?

I decided that I would say nothing to either of them because it would wreck the last three days Hugh and Beth would be in Sydney, and how would that effect their children Matt and Sophia as well.

By 4.30 that afternoon, I've calmed down enough and made the decision that I wouldn't go into the office the next day, so rang Mike. We've agreed I'd go back to the office on the following Tuesday. We'd meet first thing to discuss what would happen next but it wasn't to happen till the Wednesday.

Another ambush

That's when it got nasty, and I was to find out about the lies that had been told.

"Okay Mike, so I have to accept there's no longer a role at ABC because that's changing, so what will my redundancy package look like, and what about the commission for the PTA sale?"

"Get this straight Kevin," as Mike glared at me, his teeth clenched together as he spoke with some venom. "You won't be getting fucking commission and a redundancy package, you'll get what I'm prepared to fucking give you which is commission and that's all you'll get."

I said, "What do you mean? It was you who said there would be no more sales and marketing role. That it'd be an account management role and time would be billable to the client, that's what you fucking well said, so that tells me that the role is fucking well redundant."

"At the lunch you, Karen and Steve had last week with Peter Love from Computer Technologies, they both told me you and Peter said you falsified that fucking Request For Proposal (RFP)," Mike spat at me. "By changing the answers to some of the questions, when it was demonstrated it was a total and utter fuck up," he shouted. "I had to work three or four days in a row until 3 o'clock in the morning to fix it and it's a sale we shouldn't have won. It was a complete fucking disaster because of what you did," Mike raged.

"I could have you both charged with criminal negligence," Mike shouted at me.

"What the fuck Mike?! "So I've supposedly sat down with Computer Technologies, gone through the specs with them, and I've convinced them to lie and falsify the RFP? How fucking stupid a proposition is that?" I yelled. "How the fuck did you accept such a shower of shit from those pricks. No one here knows the Wizard system Mike, do they, fucking no one? Get those lying assholes in here right now I demanded and let's have this out right here and now."

"They're not here," said Mike.

I just found it very hard to accept that a man of Mike's intelligence would except such a crock of bullshit but there it was.

"How fucking convenient, Mike." We're both standing and facing each other, both of us looking daggers at one another.

Chapter 1 – My Story

"This meeting's over and I suggest you organize yourself to handover your accounts next week," and with that he walked out of the boardroom.

Total frustration

I walk out of the boardroom and grab my things. I could hardly contain my anger and frustration as I walked out of the office. Again, everyone who saw me averted their eyes as I walked out. They must have heard it all coming from the boardroom as Mike and I were yelling at each other.

What happened over the next two days was this; when Sandy got home I told her what had transpired in the boardroom. The accusation of falsifying the RFP, Peter and I could be charged with criminal negligence and the shouting match that had ensued. I would only be getting the PTA commission, no redundancy package, and two weeks with the outplacement people. That was it after nearly ten years.

On Thursday morning Mike asked me to sign a document agreeing that I would be paid 50% of the commission the next day and the balance in two weeks' time. The rest of the day was just a blur.

On the Friday morning, I got a phone call from Mike telling me he thought Rachel, the bookkeeper and paymistress had made a mistake with my payout and he would discuss it with her later in the day when he returned.

Mike didn't get back, and I didn't get paid. I stayed until 6.30 on the off chance that Mike would get back and the issue had been resolved, but no such luck.

It's now close to 7:00 in the evening and there's no one left in the office but me. What to do? I felt hollow, I felt sad, I felt let down, I felt lost. I was now just an afterthought and nobody in ABC gave a tuppeny fuck about me.

I walk around a completely empty office. I'm the only one here, I haven't been paid, I haven't heard from Mike and the last person here but me hasn't even bothered to divert the phones and shut the front door.

It was all I could do to hold back my emotions. I'd been here for more than nine years and here I was leaving behind me a place that I'd put my heart and soul into. I could look myself in the eye and say quite truthfully to myself that if it weren't for me, this place would no longer exist.

The final confrontation

Mike rang me at home on the Sunday. "I've just gone through the figures Kevin and been in touch with Rachel. On Monday go into the office and Rachel will give you a check and you'll get the balance in another two weeks." And with that he hung up the phone.

No goodbye, no thank you, no apologies, no good luck. Just a cold statement and a clunk as the phone went down and that was the end of that.

I felt a little stupid standing in the reception waiting for Rachel but at the same time I felt like storming into the office and telling everybody to listen to my side of the story because what they been told was a crock of bullshit.

A few moments later Rachel came out and with some paperwork in her hand and said, "Let's go into the interview room for privacy." Her tone was blunt and matter of fact. "Here is your check and this is the breakup of the total amount. Check it and sign here," she said in a demanding voice as I flicked my eyes over the items and the amounts.

"Where's my superannuation in this Rachel?" I asked.

Chapter 1 – My Story

"Superannuation?" she said in a voice full of contempt. "Superannuation? You're not getting any superannuation. You're getting what's here on this check, that's all you're getting and you don't deserve a penny more."

I picked up the check. "I need you to sign for the check Kevin." "Get stuffed" I snapped back, "I'm not signing for anything."

I was absolutely fuming as I caught the lift down to the car park. As soon as I get home I'll call Chris and get his opinion. What rights do I have?

The next sledgehammer blow

Chris was a lawyer specializing in wrongful dismissal by employers. I'd been referred to him by the daughter of a very close friend and he'd offered to help if he could.

I was in for a bit of a shock.

I stormed into the house, went into the study and picked up the phone to call Chris.

"G'day Kevin this is Chris, what's happened mate?"

I described to Chris what had happened, commission only no severance of any kind and no superannuation. "What options do you think I have Chris?" I asked.

"You're not going to like this Kevin, but if I were you I would let it go."

"Why's that?" I asked as I sucked in my breath.

"If this ever got to court, it'd be your word against his. All he'd have to say is the documents were falsified by you and Peter at Computer

Technologies, he had to retrieve the sale to save his business, and you had to go. As much as I hate to tell you this Kev, after all you've been through, my advice to you is to drop it. Just let it go and get on with your life."

"But Chris it's a lot of money to walk away from."

"Kev, it'd cost you three times as much as it's worth, to even get some kind of settlement would cost thousands, and lawyers don't come cheap."

That was the end of that.

So why have I told you all of this?

Because that two week period was to play such a significant role in what happened to me a few years later. The lesson I had to learn from it, how that applies to taking back control of your life so you can move forward, and how you can and must turn a negative into a positive.

Chapter 1 – My Story

Part Two – A Brutal and Violent Childhood

I'm seven years old.

I didn't hear the light being switched on but the light penetrated my eyes.

In a sleepy haze for a fraction of a second then the fear grips my stomach, the familiar feeling of that vomiting feeling of fear in my throat is instantly there again, my heart is pounding as I'm dragged up into the air with my upper right arm and shoulder in the vice like grip of my father's hand.

"You useless jackanapes!" he screams at me. "I told you to stand up, who said you could fall asleep?" as he smashed me backwards into the living room wall. "How dare you fall asleep!"

With my senses reeling, my heart pounding I realized I had disobeyed my father and it's another thrashing as his cupped hand smashes into my backside and my feet leave the ground.

I don't fall because I'm still in that vice-like grip as I'm shoved face first into the corner of the room. "Now you'll stand there and stay awake until I tell you, do you understand me?" he shouts.

"Yer, yer, yer, yes," I stutter, as I try to deal with the pain in my shoulder and the feeling that my buttocks are on fire from the force and power of his blows.

The living room light goes off and the room is in darkness again as I stand trembling in the corner, my eyes scrunched shut, my shoulder with piercing, searing pain, and my buttocks on fire as I try to concentrate on not falling asleep again.

What have I done this time?

My crime was that I'd taken the carborundum knife-sharpener from the kitchen, and while playing a game of pirates, it had been knocked out of my hand as we played sword fights. It hit the ground tip first and had broken around an inch down from the tip of the shaft.

The carborundum was my sword. I'd fashioned my pirate's belt out of a couple of old cleaning rags and stuck the carborundum through that and my shirt.

After the game, I came into the kitchen with my trusty sword hanging off my makeshift pirate's belt, took it out and put it back in the kitchen drawer.

It was some time after my brother and I had gone to bed and was sound asleep when my father burst into the bedroom and roughly grabbed me by the collar of my pajamas top pulling me out of bed.

He dragged me into the kitchen thrusting the broken carborundum into my face, screaming at me, "You useless good for nothing idiot. Who gave you permission to take this?"

"Nnn, nnn, nnn, no one," I stuttered.

"What the devil were you doing with it?"

"It was my sword, I was playing pirates."

"Playing pirates, you useless nincompoop," as his hand slammed into

Chapter 1 – My Story

my buttocks with such force that it lifted me, with one foot off the ground. "How did it get broken?" as his hand slammed into me again.

"I dropped it," I said, "and it broke the tip."

"How dare you take anything without permission?" he fumed. "Did you think I wouldn't find out, you useless piece of nothing?"

"Nnn, nnn, no," I stuttered again.

"You'll be punished for this and you won't do it again."

He dragged me into the living room and thrust me into the corner. "You'll stay here all night to teach you a lesson, and you will not go to sleep. If I catch you falling asleep you won't forget it for a long time," he bellowed at me. "Do you understand me, you useless jackanapes?"

"Yer, yer, yer, yes," I stuttered again.

"I don't know why I ever had you," he muttered, and with that, he walked out and turned the lights out.

I could vaguely hear my mother pleading with him to let me go back to bed, that I had been punished enough. "No, he has to learn a lesson that he can't take anything without permission to play stupid silly games."

"But he's only a little boy, playing with his friends."

"Not acceptable, and that's the end of it," he said. Then silence.

I was shivering with fear and pain… then the lights went on.

I have no idea what time it was, or how much time had passed, but I was awake and leaning on the corner wall when I heard my parent's bedroom door open, and the fear came hurtling back to me as I started to tremble, not knowing what was about to befall me.

The light went on. "Get to bed," was all he said as he walked out, turning out the light, leaving me to find my way to bed in the dark.

It wasn't the first belting I got, because there had been many of them, and it was just one of many more I was to get over the years.

My father was an absolute tyrant. Essentially, we all lived in fear of him.

There were other beatings I can recall, but two of them have stuck with me over the years because of the savagery of them.

The first was a time when I was eight or nine years old. It was a Sunday because it happened at Sunday lunch.

Earlier in the day, while mowing the grass in the back garden, I had inadvertently run over a stone which was part of a garden border. The result was the blade hitting the stone, and the stone hitting the edge of the mower and breaking a piece off, about 50 mm, or two inches or so.

I finished mowing the grass, did the last of the raking, putting the grass clippings onto the compost heap behind the garage.

With the mower on its side, I hosed it down underneath to clean the blades and the housing. With that done, I looked at the mower and knew I was going to be in trouble.

My father is inside the house in the kitchen.

Sunday lunch was a family ritual in those days. It was the day we had either roast chicken or roast lamb. It's a day I've never forgotten. I walk into the kitchen to tell my father I had finished and to tell him what

Chapter 1 – My Story

happened to the mower.

It was the calm before the storm. We walked out to the garage where I'd left the mower before putting it away. He squatted down by the mower as I showed him where the cast iron base of the mower had been smashed out by the stone.

As he got up he swung around and the back of his clenched fist slammed into the side of my head and down I went.

"You useless no good for nothing jackanapes. You useless good for nothing moron. That stupidity and carelessness has wrecked the mower. Put it away and get out of my sight until lunch is served. Get to your room and don't come out until I say so."

Sometime later, "Kevin! Kevin!" screamed my father. I come out of the bedroom my brother and I share, and go into the kitchen.

"Take the soup to the dining room and put it on the sideboard," he says.

I do as I'm bid then return to the kitchen. I can tell by the tone of his voice and the way he looks at me that I'm in trouble and I'm very much on edge.

We sit down at the table. He is at the head of the table and my mother is at the other end. I'm to my father's left, my sister Rosemarie to the left of me. Nigel, my older brother is to my father's right.

We wait for my father to start because that is the signal that the rest of us can start.

I pick up my soup spoon and dip it into the soup, making sure I obey all the rules. Not too much in the spoon, keep it level, don't slurp, you take it from the forward edge and sipping, not slurping. You tilt the spoon toward you and actually pour the soup into your mouth from the side of the spoon.

My father is watching me, waiting for the slightest mistake and I start trembling a little and my hand is shaking. I pick up the next spoonful of soup and I drop the spoon. The stem hits the edge of the soup bowl, flinging soup up into the air, over the table and the floor, as the spoon clatters to the floor.

"S… s… s… sorry", I stutter as I get up from the table to go to the kitchen and get a sink cloth to wipe up the mess on the table and floor.

With that done, I sit back down at the table, with my father watching me again, I fill my spoon with soup, but this time I'm quite visibly shaking. The spoon slips out of my hand again, and again, falls to the floor. Soup all over the table and dripping down and onto the floor. Again, I apologize and go through the same process.

There is a total silence in the dining room as my sister, brother, mother and father watch me as I scurry into the kitchen with the sink cloth covered in soup. I rinse it then go back to the table.

I sit down and attempt to start again.

This time it's as if the spoon has a mind of its own. I pick it up, go to get it into the soup and just drop it. That's how much I'm shaking. It goes straight into the soup bowl, splashing soup over the table.

That's when my father explodes. "What the devil, what's wrong with you, you good for nothing idiot?" as his hand smashes into my ear.

He leaps out of his chair and grabs me with the shoulder of my shirt and my upper arm, pulling me off my chair. "What's wrong with you?" he screams at me. "Why can't you control yourself you useless jackanapes."

Chapter 1 – My Story

My mother appeals to him, "David darling, he's just so afraid, please don't do this to him."

"No, he has to learn how to control himself," he shouts back.

He drags me out of the dining room and through the kitchen into the back vestibule, pushing my back into the brick wall below the kitchen window with the whole force of his upper body behind his hands, which had twisted my shirt up into balls in his fists, as he punches into my chest to emphasize his words as he bellows at me.

"You're damned useless, you can't control your manners at the dining table and you can't even do a simple task like mowing the lawn without smashing the mower because you are so careless and stupid."

Smash, as he backhands me across the face with such force that the left side of my face smashes into the brick wall causing me to bite my cheek as I feel the sharp pain of it and the taste of blood in my mouth.

He pushes me backwards towards the door of the bedroom, slamming me back first into the door frame.

I can't remember what I was thinking, but I remember the stinging in my mouth, the heat in my cheeks, the dull pain in my chest, and a feeling of helplessness.

He shoved me into the bedroom with such force that I fell backwards, hitting the back of my head on the upright of the double bunk bed.

"Don't come out until I tell you, you useless waster," as he slammed the door shut behind him.

I pick myself up and almost trip the last couple of steps as I flop onto the bed. My eyes are stinging from the effort I put into shutting out the pain. The only thing I can remember feeling is one of bewilderment.

I'm lying down on the bed, shaking and wondering how long this can possibly last.

It seems like an age has past when my mother comes into the room and puts her hand on my shoulder. "Come into the kitchen and have your lunch."

It seems that there is virtually nothing I can do to stop the beatings, the words that flay me, and the fear that comes to me every day.

But the one thing I promised myself that he will never do to me, is to make me cry.

Little did I know at the time, but those formative years are the ones that had set my personality in stone for the rest of my life.

They had set the structure of my subconscious mind, my very persona, and most of all, those two little voices in my head… the negative one, and the positive one.

As a result, the rest of my life would follow.

What do the experts say?

All the scientific research, and all the anecdotal evidence says that your personality, the pattern of your subconscious mind, and what shapes you for the rest of your life, is formed within the first 12 years of your life.

So here I was, right at the cusp of that. A useless waster who would never amount to anything.

Where to now in life?

Well, fuck you, I will amount to something. It might take years, but fuck you, it will happen.

Chapter 1 – My Story

Part Three – My Father

There's no doubt in my mind, through my own life's experience, and the knowledge I now have, that my father suffered with PTSD because of his violent childhood and his experiences during WW2.

My father was like a chameleon, and just like a chameleon, he could 'change colors' in an instant.

One moment, charming, then in the next fraction of a second, explode into a fit of rage that could see him lash out physically, or in a verbal tirade with an acid tongue, vitriolic in its use of words to flay you and make you feel worthless.

What was it that had happened to him to make my father such a violent person that he could hit his children with such force that it would knock them off their feet?

What was it in his upbringing that made him this way?

His father, my paternal grandfather, was a self-made man, but not a nice one. Essentially, he was what was known as a loan shark. He loaned people money at exorbitant interest rates and deliberately targeted poorer people because he could frighten, intimidate, and manipulate them more easily.

As a result, he became very rich, but also, he had no compunction in bashing his sons.

It was my father who bore the brunt of his father's physical and verbal abuse, a father who would not tolerate not being obeyed, very much like he was to become himself.

My father left home at 16 to become an apprentice motor mechanic with Morris Garages of England, a company that is now defunct, but in those days was a major British car manufacturer.

My grandfather wanted his sons to become doctors or lawyers. He wanted them to be respectable, and as a result, he too would become respectable.

Both Geoffrey and Howard went on to become doctors. Geoffrey became a heart specialist, and Howard, a well respected GP, and they both married doctors too, which really pleased my grandfather.

When WW2 broke out, my father joined the Army. He went into the Royal Army Service Corps, (RASC). He was at Dunkirk when the British forces were driven from Europe by Hitler. He then went to the Middle East. He was wounded in action and it was here, while in hospital in 1942, that he met Josephine Jean Busby Masson, the lady who became my mother.

Jean, as she was commonly called, was a VAD nurse, (Voluntary Aid Detachment), a part of the Royal Australian Army Nursing Corps. She and her two sisters, Geraldine and Robyn, had been brought up in Palestine between the two world wars.

Her father Gerald Masson, at the outbreak of World War I, enlisted in the Australian Army. His army number was 151. As an expert horseman, he became a member of A Squadron, the 9th Light Horse Regiment. He landed at Anzac Cove Gallipoli on 25 April 1915, straight into the

Chapter 1 – My Story

hellhole of that day where over 2000 Australians and New Zealanders were killed or wounded in action.

He was then posted to the Middle East where he saw a lot of action, and he participated in the last major cavalry charge of World War I, the "Charge at Beersheba."

As a part of the Anzac Mounted Division, a part of the Desert Mounted Corps, Captain Gerry Masson, MID, was with Lord Allenby at the Battle of Jaffa, and walked through the Jaffa Gate into the old city of Jerusalem with Allenby on the 11th December, 1917.

Gerry fell in love with the Middle East, and it was while in Cairo in Egypt that he met his future wife Jessie Andrews, an Australian Army nurse. It was in Jerusalem in 1919 that he took his discharge from the Australian Army, and the very next day he became the Chief Agricultural Officer of the Palestine government. T E Lawrence, or Lawrence of Arabia as he was known, met Gerry during the war and he and Gerry became very good friends. Their friendship continued afterwards with Lawrence being a frequent guest. They didn't mind a drink or three either.

What a contrast between the two families. My mother's, one of love and stability, my father's, a dysfunctional one of physical, verbal and mental violence.

Part Four – You're Not Allowed To Succeed

How dare you be good at anything!

At high school, I was not a good student. My favorite subjects were English, History, Social Studies and Geography. Math, Algebra, Geometry and the sciences were too complicated for me.

1962 was a watershed year for me as a student. I was doing poorly. At home, because of this, there was constant criticism from my father. My end of year result in the subjects I liked was pretty good. The others were poor, and the response from my father to my report card was a tirade of abuse and of how stupid I was. What was it that I didn't get about doing well at school, and why was I wasting time with football and swimming?

As a swimmer, I had made the Victorian school boys swimming team. In breaststroke, I made the semifinals, in the 100 m freestyle I finished last in the final, and didn't make the cut for diving. For someone who had absolutely no formal swimming or diving training, I felt I had done pretty well.

The other good part of that year was I made the school football team. Towards the end of the football season we played Melbourne High School, an elite state run high school. In a game where we were the underdogs, we beat them convincingly, and I played the best game of my young life. It was just a blinder, and it was as if the ball was attracted to me.

Chapter 1 – My Story

At that match was a St Kilda talent scout. Along with another of our players whose name I don't remember, we were asked if we would like to try out with one of the St Kilda age-based teams. Not bad at 14. I went on to play a handful of games with the Under 19 side.

To my father, there was no element of success in any of this. It was purely a waste of time. With money extremely tight, home life was awful and I had no motivation. I felt totally unloved and worthless and I just wanted to leave school. So, with my parent's agreement I left school at the end of the year.

Part Five – Joining the Australian Regular Army

In 1966, the family was living in Lane Cove West, where my parents rented a modest three-bedroom cottage.

A few weeks short of my 17th birthday, while waiting at the bus stop one day to catch the bus to work, I noticed an advertisement, and it gave me an idea.

It was just bloody brilliant! I could get a trade. How good was that?

Here was the way I could get away from home, get away from my father, get away from the abuse, the acid tongue, the constant criticism, being made to feel insignificant and worthless.

I could get away from my father, get away from the abuse and give myself some direction in life?

So that's just exactly what I set out to do.

I took a day off work and went into the Army Recruiting Office which was in York Street in the city to find out what I had to do to get into the Army. I sat down with the Recruiting Sergeant and he took me through all the tests and processes that I would have to do to get to the point where the Army would accept me as a recruit. I got started that very day.

I made the decision not to tell my parents until I had to, because I did not want them to say no, most particularly my father.

I did everything necessary to get accepted. All the tests, all the evaluations, just everything that was required of me so I could start my new life. It would take about ten days, and I would be advised by letter, so I asked if I could call in at the end of that time, and get the letter from them. Ten days later, that's what I did.

I could hardly contain my excitement as I opened the envelope, and there it was. Yes, I had been accepted. All that was then needed was my parents' signature on the appropriate forms.

I still have a reasonable recall of the day when I got home from work, told my parents how I had decided to join the Australian Army, and all I needed was their signature. There was genuine shock, genuine surprise, and for the first time I could ever remember receiving it, I could recall my father's genuine satisfaction with something I had done. He was all for it, and was happy to sign the papers.

The 13th of March 1966 was to be my first day as an Army recruit, and the Vietnam war was well and truly on. I had to be at the Eastern Command Personnel Depot at Watsons Bay at 9 am that day, and boy oh boy was I happy. You bet I was!

Chapter 1 – My Story

My father drove me there. As I got out of the car to open the boot and get my bag with the personal possessions I had been instructed to have with me, he put his hand on my shoulder and wished me well.

He got out of the car, then came over to me and gave me a hug. It was the first piece of tenderness I had got from him in what must have been years, because I could not recall the previous time he'd shown any affection towards me.

How did I feel?

On the outside I was feeling cool and calm and looking forward to what lay ahead of me.

Inside I was just so relieved. It was a feeling of massive excitement. You know the one? It's the one that screams out yes! yes! yes!

Free, free, free! I'm finally fucking free!

Basic training – the start to the vital part of the conditioning process

In those days, Kapooka, just out of Wagga Wagga, about 400 kms south of Sydney, was the basic training center for Regular Army soldiers.

Basic training is the starting point of the process of shaping the human response to stress. Fight or flight, with the fighting response being required by the military. Our brains and our minds being trained and conditioned to make us act instinctively, an instantaneous reaction which we don't even think about, such is the level of our conditioning. It's how the military train men to activate the fight response when an order is given, or a shot is fired. It ensures we will instinctively react with discipline and together as a team, and we won't even think about it.

After drill and weapons training to hone our instant responses, there was the physical training part of our time. We were brought to the peak of physical fitness. When you put all this together, the military requires men and women who have personal, physical, and mental discipline and can work as part of a team.

When joining the Army I had decided I wanted to get a trade, but that was not to be. I had wanted to go to the Signal Corps, or what is called RAEME, which is the Corps of Electrical and Mechanical Engineers.

The Australian Army had been involved in Vietnam since 1960 when it sent advisors to help train the South Vietnamese Army. By early 1965 the war was escalating and the Australian government agreed to send a battalion group and support Arms to Vietnam to support the South Vietnamese and American war effort.

I was posted to the Corps of Infantry, as were most of my colleagues. This meant I would go to Ingleburn in south-western Sydney where the Regular Army School of Infantry was located. My first reaction was one of total disappointment. But now that I was going to Infantry my thoughts where all on the Vietnam war. Is that where I would end up?

Infantry Corps Training

It would be three months of intensive training. A lot of time spent on weapons, and a lot of time on tactics, patrolling and ambush skills.

As our infantry corps training was coming to an end, we would soon find out what our next postings were to be.

When that time arrived, I was posted, along with several of my colleagues, to the Second Battalion of the Royal Australian Regiment based at Ennogera, a suburb of Brisbane in Queensland.

Chapter 1 – My Story

Now a real soldier

I remember quite clearly the big sign at Roma Station saying 'Welcome to Sunny Queensland' but it was pissing down rain like a tropical downpour. So much for sunny Queensland!

On arriving at Battalion Headquarters we went in and handed in our paperwork. My posting was to the Administration Company which I was pretty unhappy about but could do nothing so I just had to take it on the chin. I was assigned as a clerk in the company headquarters, and commenced what to me was a boring and mundane job.

The battalion had been warned for duty in Vietnam and was to embark for South Vietnam in May 1967. The months immediately prior to that were taken up by a lot of training. There was a battalion exercise in Tin Can Bay in Queensland then the battalion was put through the Jungle Training Centre at Canungra.

The battalions final exercise was at Shoalwater Bay, just north of Rockhampton. At about this time the 2IC of Admin Company did not want me to go to Vietnam with the battalion because he thought I was too young.

For me that was like red rag to a bull and I asked for an immediate transfer to a Rifle Company. This was granted, and I was posted to A Company.

At that time the only available role for me was to be the Batman for the Company 2 IC, Captain Kevin Grayson, or 'Skinny' as he was known to everyone. At least I was in a Rifle Company and away from the boring bullshit of paperwork.

Skinny was a great bloke and very easy to work for. He had been in Korea, Borneo and Malaya, and had then done what was known as a 'Knife and Fork' course to become an officer.

Part Six – Vietnam, Here We Come

With all the battalion training over I found that, being Skinny's Batman I would be going with him as part of the company advance party.

Two weeks later I landed in Vietnam. It was two weeks, less a day, after my 19th birthday, on 13th May 1967.

The purpose of the advance party was to be able to work with the battalion that was about to depart Vietnam, so there was a smooth handover and it would be an easy transition when the main part of the battalion arrived.

I'm not quite sure how long the time frame was after the Company arrived in Vietnam, but A Company was the first company of our battalion to do its six weeks rotation at the Horseshoe. The Horseshoe was called that because it was a hill the shape of a horseshoe, an old volcanic cone that was a feature overlooking miles and miles of rice paddies not far from the village of Dat Do.

It was a fortified hill where the platoons of the company lived underground in sandbagged bunkers which were connected right round the perimeter by sandbagged trenches for protection from mortar attack. There was a battery of 105 howitzers in the middle of the feature and their role was as fire protection for patrols from the Horseshoe or from the Task Force base at Nui Dat.

The Horseshoe was surrounded by barbed wire fences and a minefield for protection against a physical assault by the Viet Cong. Along with that there was a responsibility, on a daily basis, to man a checkpoint at one entrance to the village of Dat Do while the South Vietnamese

Chapter 1 – My Story

Army (ARVN), manned one at the other end of the village. The platoons regularly patrolled around the Horseshoe, and two- to three-day ambush patrols were all part of daily life.

It was only a week or so after getting to the Horseshoe that I told Skinny I wanted to go to one of the platoons. He was quite okay with this, telling me it could happen as soon as an opening came up, and that happened within a couple of days.

That's how I came to get to be in 2 Section of 1 Platoon.

The Platoon Commander was Lieutenant Vic Adams, a graduate of the Royal Military College at Duntroon and an absolute born leader who had the total respect of every member of the platoon.

The Platoon Sergeant was Ron Melling, and he too was an excellent soldier and leader, and in my opinion, we were so lucky to have great Section Commanders in Ken 'Tojo' O'Doherty, Max Schmidt, and my Section Commander, Geoff Alexander. I don't know what it was about it, but we just seemed to be blessed with great leadership, and it was just as if we were a great bunch of mates who happened to be an infantry platoon into the bargain.

Our Company Commander was Major Peter 'Jack' White, also a Duntroon graduate, and again hugely admired and respected as an excellent Company Commander. He could be really tough on you if you stepped out of line, but once it was done it was done.

1 Platoon

I became the Section Machine-Gunner when one of the guys made the decision he had reached a boundary which he was not able to go beyond. He'd had enough, and told Vic Adams he couldn't continue on without putting his mates in danger.

It took a great deal of courage to do that.

It takes really serious courage to recognize and admit to yourself that you've reached a boundary, then take action to do something about it for the benefit of your mates.

There were some who called him a coward, but what he did was not cowardice, not by any measure of it. What he did was to look after his mates. That, to me, took a shitload of guts, and I'll call him a mate forever.

So, with my massive height of 5'6" and huge weight and muscular physique of about 10 stone 7, I was the perfect candidate. No wonder I got to be the machine-gunner!

Mateship ending in tragedy

R & R (Rest and Recuperation) Leave of five days was the only time you could actually get out of the country and leave the Vietnam war behind, and there was a choice of Taipei, Singapore, Hong Kong, Bangkok or Sydney.

I chose to go to Singapore. Don't know why but that was my choice and what an adventure it was. Apart from Vietnam, Singapore was to be the first foreign country I'd been to.

It was after the shit-fight that was Tet, 1968, and with excitement on my scheduled day of departure that I got dressed in my summer uniform, grabbed my Army travel bag packed with the few civilian clothes I had, made my way to Company Headquarters to get the duty vehicle which would take me down to Luscombe Airfield.

From Luscombe I would catch a Caribou aircraft which would take me to Saigon. An overnight stay in Saigon at the US transit center at Bien

Chapter 1 – My Story

Hoa Air Base, and the next day a charter flight on a civilian aircraft to Singapore.

What luxury, sitting in a very comfortable seat, being able to order a cold beer and really looking forward to five days in a city that I'd only read about.

I was only one of two Australians on the plane and I was seated next to an African American. He was a massive man, and I could see he was US Special Forces. We introduced ourselves and started chatting. He had never met anyone from Australia before, and until we met he didn't know there were Australian forces in Vietnam, had only heard of Australia but knew nothing about it.

We hit it off straight away and as he looked about around the plane, he told me he could not see many other combat soldiers and we should get together in Singapore and have a few beers if I was okay with that, which I was. It was only when he stood up that I realized just how big he was. Shit he was big! It turned out he was 6'10" tall and weighed 17-plus stone, but what a bloody nice bloke.

We get to Singapore and once we'd got through customs and immigration we were ushered into a conference room where we were briefed on what was expected of us while in Singapore as visitors, where we would be staying, the local customs and the inevitable warnings about venereal disease and staying out of trouble.

We were then told which hotels we would be going to and it turned out that Dan and I were going to the same hotel which suited us both down to the ground. We agreed to meet at the bar as soon as we had settled into our rooms so we could have a beer and make some plans for what we would do over the next few days.

We were here for a good time, because any day back there you could be dead and pushing up daisies, so let's get into it! It was a kaleidoscope of bars, girls, sightseeing, more bars, more girls, a little bit more sightseeing more bars again, more girls, a little bit of shopping, and so it went on.

It seemed that everywhere we went, people would just stare at us. It was a real sight to behold. Can you just imagine it? Here's Dan, a bloody great giant of a man, walking around with beautiful oriental girls who didn't even come up to his armpit, and here's short-ass me with a girl on my arm, and the man mountain that was Dan. Fucking priceless!

It seemed our days were spent in an almost alcoholic haze of just having a blast and letting our hair down because you never knew what was around the corner.

But, as they say in the classics, all good things must come to an end and it was time to leave Singapore and to head back to the shit-hole of the war in Vietnam.

By the time Dan and I got on the plane for our flight back to Vietnam we were absolutely wiped out. Between us we had spent over US$3,000 which was a shitload of money in those days. To show for it, Dan had two T-shirts and I had a sports coat and a T-shirt.

We had an absolute blast together and no regrets, became dead-set mates, and agreed to stay in contact and swapped military and home addresses. We both wrote to one another very soon after we got back and Dan sent me a US Special Forces knife which he had said he could get for me. I still have that knife, and it's still as sharp as a razor. Each time I look at it, it brings back the memories.

Sadly, about six weeks later I got a letter from his commanding officer. Dan had been severely wounded when his unit was caught in an ambush

Chapter 1 – My Story

and he didn't make it. What made it worse was that I got the letter when we were out on an operation, and there was nowhere to hide so I could let go of my grief. Fuck this rotten war! And that night in my hutchie, alone with my thoughts in the darkness, I cried as silently as I could. Fuck it was hard.

It took many weeks for the memories to start to fade. It was almost as if Dan was a shadow by my side looking over me and looking out for me.

In 2013 I visited The Wall in Washington DC. I found his name, put my hand on it, and it was as if we were together again. I couldn't contain my emotions as the tears started rolling down my cheeks.

As I thought back over the time we spent in Singapore, the girls, the bars, the little bit of shopping, the little bit of sightseeing, it all came back to me as I'm half laughing and half crying, recalling the antics we got up to. The times we were sitting in a bar, half pissed, laughing our heads off at some silly joke, and I'm trembling a little as I try to wipe away the constantly falling tears. Fuck the war.

I was deliberately wearing a jacket and my campaign medals, when a beautiful thing happened. A group of three young girls approached me and asked me if I was a veteran. I told them I was, that I was an Australian Vietnam veteran, and I was here to pay my respects to my very good mate Dan and to all of those whose names are on the wall for the sacrifice they had made.

They then handed me a little packet which I still have.

I've sometimes wondered where they are now. If you are one of those three lovely and beautiful young ladies, I hope this finds you well and happy. It was a lovely gesture.

Going Home!

And then going home was just around the corner.

2 RAR/NZ Anzac was to be relieved by 4 RAR, and it would become 4 RAR/NZ Anzac.

Three and a-wakey, two and a-wakey, one and a-wakey, then it was the big day.

One of the benefits of going over to Vietnam on the advance party was that I would come back to Australia in the advance party.

Going over to Vietnam we had gone by Hercules transport but coming back, oh what a luxury, it was aboard a Qantas Boeing 707.

Because of the unpopularity of the war and the risk of protesters we got off the plane well short of the main terminal and out of sight of regular

Chapter 1 – My Story

passengers. It was a freezing cold hangar and in the time it took to clear customs, get luggage, get leave passes, and actually leave the hangar, I was freezing bloody cold.

There were my parents to greet me and there were hugs all around. As we walked towards where the family car was parked I was so cold I cramped up and couldn't walk. It was one of those rare times where my father showed any affection. He literally picked me up and piggybacked me to the car.

For the next six weeks I was on post combat leave, giving me the time to unwind from living on the edge 24/7 for almost all of the previous 12 months.

Back to the Battalion

All too soon my leave was over and I had to catch the train back to 2 RAR at Ennogera, and get back into harness.

Skinny Grayson was back from leave and was the acting Company Commander.

The routine for the next few days was sprucing up the company area giving the barracks building a spring clean and generally keeping busy. During the day, this meant digging up the gardens, turning over the soil, mowing grass and then laying tons and tons of topsoil.

Pretty boring and mind numbing after the last 12 months but that's the way it was.

A life-changing decision

If you could describe how I felt about life at the time it was just humdrum boring mindless crap, and I had hardly any motivation at all. That's when I made the decision to go back to Vietnam. That decision was to set in train some very significant events in my life.

The next morning I went down to company headquarters and asked the Company Clerk to ask Skinny Grayson if I can speak with him. I was invited to go into his office.

"What is it Kev?" I told him I'd made a decision to go back to Vietnam as a reinforcement. "You must be fucking crazy Kev. What the fuck do you want to do that for? You got a fucking death wish or what?" And we both laughed at that.

"No sir, I just want to go back." "OK Kev, I'll get the paperwork sorted."

That weekend I drove down to Sydney to tell my parents about the decision I'd made.

My father took my announcement calmly. "Why do you want to do that Kevin?" The only thing that I can think of to say is, "Because I want to and I'm a soldier." He nodded. "I see, so when is this going to happen?" "I'd expect I'll be back there around November sometime." "Well, that's your decision and it's yours to make." With that he fell silent.

To say that my mother was upset would be an understatement. Within moments she was in tears. "Why do you want to go back to the hellhole of Vietnam she cried out to me. Why? Haven't you had enough?"

She put her arms around me and as she put her face next to mine, her tears wet both of our cheeks and I could feel her trembling. It wasn't something to be enjoyed, but my decision was made.

The next little adventure

It was one morning while on our usual daily parade that Skinny came out to address us. "Is there anyone here who has a Surf Bronze lifesaving certificate." I was the only one to immediately stick my hand in the air, and said yes I do, because I did.

Chapter 1 – My Story

With the parade over, I walked over to company HQ and asked to see Skinny to find out more about what having a Surf Bronze meant.

Two companies of Royal Marine commandos based in Singapore on the Navy's troop carrier, HMS *Bulwark*, had been in Queensland acting as the enemy for the next battalion of Australian troops to go to Vietnam. They were going to be rotated through the national fitness camp at Tallebudgera on the Gold Coast, and for their safety the Army needed to provide lifeguards on the beach, hence the requirement for the Surf Bronze, and now I'm a lifeguard.

Local businesses were offering things like discount offers for lunches and dinners, discounted sightseeing tours and free tickets to local attractions. One of these was the Water Ski Gardens on the Nerang River, who ran a Saturday night dance.

That sounded pretty good to me, so on the first Saturday night, and because I had my own car I was able to take four of the Brits with me.

Part Seven – My Life is About to Change

That Saturday night was to be one of the most significant nights of my life.

About four or five tables away from where we were sitting I noticed a girl who seemed to keep looking at me. She was very pretty. No, wrong. She looked drop-dead gorgeous to me. On a number of occasions she had been approached by guys asking her to dance but she had knocked them all back.

And still she's kept looking at me, then she gave me a half smile. With that I thought there's only one of two things that can happen. She will either get up and have a dance with me, or she won't.

"Hi I'm Kevin, would you like to have a dance?" I asked. "Yes okay" was the answer. As we walked towards the dance floor, I asked her what her name was, "I'm Sandra" she said. Then I said "I noticed you looking at me a number of times, then you smiled. I was looking at you because you looked very much like the boyfriend of one of my closest girlfriends, and in this dim light it was a little difficult to tell."

This girl is just downright beautiful and I'd love to see her again.

For me this is going to be a little bit difficult. I've only been back from Vietnam a couple of months, the Vietnam war is a very divisive issue in Australia, I'm about to go again, so what do I say? It's a tough question. I decided not to tell Sandra about me being in the Army. Why ruin a good thing?! When she asked me what I did, I told her I was a lifeguard.

Sandra and I seemed to hit it off and we saw each other every day that I wasn't working on the beach and most nights. It seemed like something was starting to happen and we were really enjoying each other's company.

We had fallen for one another in the ten or so days we had been together, and we both knew it, so this was difficult.

I knew I was coming to Sydney alright because I'd be on pre-embarkation leave. But here's my dilemma. Sandra has no idea I'm in the Army, let alone in the infantry and I'll be gone for 12 months. If shit happens, I could be coming home in a coffin, or smashed up.

Chapter 1 – My Story

The time finally came when I had to take Sandra back to the Sunset Strip guesthouse where she was staying, and I had to get back to Tallabudgera before the gates were closed at midnight. It was a passionate but sad parting.

Sandra left the next day by bus for Sydney and there were only three or four more days before all of the Brits had gone through the national fitness camp and I was back to Ennogera and 2 RAR.

Things started to move rapidly.

Turning around of the lie

Here I was, madly in love and in an absolute quandary. How was I going to tell this beautiful young girl what I was about to go and do?

What would she say? What would she do?

The day after I got to Sydney and got settled at the reinforcement wing I rang her.

"Hello, this is Sandra, how can I help you?" "Hello Sandra, this is Kevin, the Kevin from the Gold Coast. I'm now in Sydney, and like I said, I'd ring you to let you know I was here."

It was almost like oh uh, umm, oh it is you. "You've taken me by surprise, are you really in Sydney?" "Yes I am" I said "and now you know I'm here I'd love to be able to see you again if you'd like to do that. Could we meet on Thursday night? Would that be okay with you?"

"I'd love to" she said. "How long are you here for?" "I'm not sure at the moment, it depends on a couple of decisions that are made over the next few days and then I'll know" I said.

I still had to find a way, and what I thought was good timing to tell her about who I really was, that I was in the Army and going back to Vietnam. I decided I'd tell her on the Thursday night. It would be as good a time as any. One way or another, it had to be done.

Either one of two things would happen. She would accept it, or she'd tell me to bugger off and it would all be over.

It was with a bit of fear and trepidation on the one hand, and excitement on the other that I waited at the main entrance of the shopping center where we had agreed to meet. Then she was walking towards me. She looked absolutely stunning.

We found a place to have a cup of coffee. The coffees arrived, and as we held hands, I drew a deep breath. "I've got something to tell you about me, and I hope you'll accept it and want to keep seeing me." She looked at me a bit quizzically, then said, "What is it?"

"I'm not a professional lifeguard. I'm a soldier in the Australian Army and I'm about to go back to Vietnam within the next three to four weeks on my second tour of duty." Her initial reaction was one of shock and surprise and there was a brief moment of silence. "Why didn't you tell me when we first met?"

"Because the war is so unpopular, I've experienced firsthand what's like to be spat on. I fell in love with you but didn't know how to tell you, so I didn't."

She leaned across to me put her arms around my neck. "Of course I still want to see you. I don't care if you're a soldier, it's us that's important, not what you do for a living" as she leaned further forward and kissed me on the lips. "I think I love you too."

Chapter 1 – My Story

You can imagine what it must have felt like to be me at that time. Here was this beautiful girl telling me she loved me and didn't care that I was a soldier.

After meeting her parents, the only thing that niggled on my mind was Sandy telling her parents, as her father most particularly, was concerned about her getting involved with a soldier, and what might happen to me in Vietnam.

Vietnam, here I come again: the last week or two

For my mother, it was a tough time too.

Two sons in Vietnam, both in the Infantry, the war escalating with the US sending more and more men to fight, and every night on television on every evening news bulletin, were stories from Vietnam.

Sandy was a bit nervous about meeting my parents for the first time. I reassured her that everything would be okay and she should relax and just be herself. They welcomed her with complete sincerity and did everything they could to assure her she was welcome and they would love to have her come over and spend time with them.

This warm welcome made her feel more comfortable as she told me later. It had helped calm her nerves. My parents did indeed take an instant liking to her, and welcomed her with open arms to their home and family. My brothers and sisters fell in love with her too.

We spent every evening together we could, and the two weekends before the week of my departure. We were madly in love.

Who knows what the next 12 months could bring?

In no time at all the day of departure arrived. I had to spend the last two nights, the Tuesday and Wednesday, at the Reinforcement Wing, and on the Thursday morning we were bussed to the Richmond Air Force Base.

Once the formalities of our departure were done, we had an hour or so to spend with family and friends before boarding the Hercules transport aircraft that would take us to Malaya, then on to South Vietnam.

It was a pretty tough hour for my parents and brother and sister. This was the second time we'd said goodbye with Vietnam the destination. It was far more tough for Sandy. At first she was able to hold back her emotions but when the announcement was made that we had to start boarding in 15 minutes, it really hit home and she started to cry. Once more I was heading off to war and our only contact would be by letter.

The announcement came and I had to go. It was a handshake from my father who wished me well and stay safe, a tearful hug and kiss from my mother and from my brother and sister.

They stepped away to give Sandy and me a moment together. Sandy was trembling and her tears flowing freely. We hugged each other very tight, and told each other we loved each other, a final kiss, and I had to walk away. I had a lump in my throat.

I didn't turn around. Goodbyes had been done so no turning back.

Back to the future

Our destination was the 1st Australian Reinforcement Unit (1 ARU).

All Infantry Corps reinforcements, no matter what their rank have to

Chapter 1 – My Story

pass through this unit. It was predominantly, private soldiers, and all NCO ranks, and mainly junior officers being 2nd Lieutenants, and the odd Lieutenant.

The purpose in doing this was to introduce soldiers to the reality of being in a war zone and all that this entails. All ranks were taken through a very specific training process and 1 ARU, as a unit had responsibility for a part of the task force perimeter.

This means picket duty at night with live ammunition in case of enemy attack, so it's down to the serious business of being ready for anything, and now we're playing for keeps.

My first promotion

About two weeks into being at 1 ARU, I was called into the CO's office, and told I was to be promoted to Lance Corporal, and stay on at 1 ARU to be trained as an Instructor.

It was totally unexpected. I asked, "Why me, when there are other NCOs here as reinforcements?" The Battalions were short of experienced NCOs, and they would be posted quickly. It was an opportunity for me with the experience I would gain at 1 ARU.

Little did I know that it wasn't to last too long.

I was the Patrol Commander taking out a one night ambush patrol. One of the men in the patrol was a 2nd Lieutenant. Unfortunately, he was one of those smartass officers you come across from time to time. He'd been in Vietnam for ten days at most, and was one of those people who knew it all. He constantly questioned my actions, telling me what he thought I should be doing.

I reminded him that I was the Patrol Commander and, although an officer, he was still a trainee, and he knew this for the purposes of field training. He took offence at this, reminding me that I was a Lance Corporal and he was an Officer. At first I ignored it, but his comments were really starting to irritate me. He would break formation to question me.

I deliberately stopped the patrol for a ten minute smoko, called him aside, and said something like, "If this doesn't stop I'll radio the duty officer at 1 ARU, have him get the CO, and have the CO clarify who's in the command of this patrol."

At the debrief when we got back I told the Duty Officer what had happened and how it concerned me. Should I speak to the OC about what had happened, or how should we handle it? The Duty Officer would raise it with the OC, and if there were any issues the OC may want to speak with me.

So that's where it ended, or so I thought.

A few days later I'm in the OR's mess one night and in comes the duty officer. It's the same 2nd Lieutenant. Too loudly I said, "Here comes General Custer," and he took offence to it. A short little 'discussion' followed and I said more than I should have. The outcome was being charged with insubordination.

I can understand the OC being caught between a rock and a hard place. I've never forgotten what he said: You'll do better work in a battalion as a private soldier. Charge dismissed.

D Company, 4 RAR

Two days later I was posted to D Company, 4 RAR as a private soldier, and allocated to 10 Platoon.

Chapter 1 – My Story

The Company Commander of D Company was Major John 'Sharky' Deighton. There were a number of us posted to D Company at the same time. We were all welcomed to the Company by him personally, which impressed me, and he spoke to us each individually and privately in his office.

In May, 1969, 4 RAR/NZ Anzac was in 'Going home to Australia' mode with little operational activity as they prepared to hand over to 6 RAR who would be doing the battalion's second tour of duty in Vietnam.

Part Eight – The Only War Story

I escaped death or wounding on a number of occasions, but those are stories for another time and place.

In war, as soldiers, we see things, do things, experience things, and we're ordered to do things, and some of these things, no man or woman should be subjected to in a civilized world.

But war is a filthy, stinking, uncivilized business, and things happen that you wish didn't. And when you think back about it later, you sometimes wish the fuck you weren't there when it did. This is what happens in war, and we're left to deal with it and live with it for the rest of our lives.

No matter how hard you try, it's always there, maybe not at the forefront of your mind that often, but sometimes circumstance brings it back from those deep, deep recesses of your subconscious mind where you wish to fuck it would remain buried forever.

As 4 RAR prepared to go home, 39 of us regular Army soldiers, reinforcements to 4 RAR who did not serve six months or more with the Battalion were posted to Headquarters Company, 1 ATF (1st Australian Task Force).

Within the official structure of headquarters company was a D and E (Defence and Employment) Platoon. This platoon was on what is known as the official Order of Battle (ORBAT). Its official role was protection for task force HQ when out in the field. At that time, mid-1969, the Task Force was commanded by Brigadier Sandy Pearson, the OC headquarters company was Major George Pratt, and they made the decision to form us into a second, but unofficial D&E Platoon.

The story of that platoon was to play a significant part in my life between 2007 and 2008 when I was still on the rollercoaster ride of a 'previous life,' the one I lived it before I made the decision to take back control of it. I was a section commander in that platoon.

The significance of it was the two-year battle four of us fought with the Australian Government and The Australian War Memorial (AWM), for the formal recognition of the platoon, it's formal recognition in the official history of Australia's involvement in the Vietnam war which was being written at the time by an historian at the AWM, and its recognition by the Australian government. We were going to be referred to as an "ad hoc infantry section," not as a platoon. The focus was to be on 2 Troop, 3rd Cavalry Regiment. Not acceptable to us, hence the fight.

In its very short but very significant existence, the second, and unofficial, D&E Platoon became very controversial and was disbanded some five weeks or thereabouts after its formation. Within that time it operated as a mechanized ready-reaction and long-range reconnaissance platoon operating completely independently of the official D&E platoon, which was operating in a totally different part of the province at the time of the controversy.

Chapter 1 – My Story

In what became known as the battle at Thua Tich, our platoon with a section of armoured personnel carriers, and a detachment of Mortars from 5 RAR, on the night of 29 May, 1969, ambushed a force of about 700 to 800 North Vietnamese and Vietcong. If they had realized just how small a force we were and surrounded us, we would have been wiped out.

It was the afternoon of the battle I first met up in Vietnam with my brother Nigel. He was the signaller for the 5 RAR Mortar detachment with us because we were operating outside the range of Artillery. Neither one of us knew the other would be there. What a coincidence.

There were two events that caused the controversy, and ultimately the disbandment of the platoon. The first was the "engineer's burial" of the bodies we found the next morning.

The second, and not known to us at the time, a request, agreed to by a person at Task Force headquarters, who has never been identified and who agreed to a request from the village chief of Xuyen Moc to dump some of the bodies in the village square for propaganda purposes. These bodies were tied to the back of one of the APC's.

On the way to Xuyen Moc, we were ambushed ourselves by the remnants of the force we'd ambushed the night before. We then proceeded to Xuyen Moc, leaving the bodies in the village square as requested.

It was just over two weeks later that the platoon was disbanded, with no explanation of any kind. Most of the men were posted to rifle companies in 9 RAR, three or four went to the official D&E Platoon, and I was posted back to 1 ARU.

It wasn't until the period of late 2007 and into 2008 that we discovered the platoon had been disbanded on the orders of the then Chief of

Army when he heard about the ambush, and saw camera footage and photographs taken at the scene of the ambush and in the Village Square at Xuyen Moc.

It took a threat to take our story to the media for the AWM and the government to take us seriously. The minister for defence, Joel Fitzgibbon, asked Mike Kelly, a former Army Colonel, and a lawyer, as the parliamentary secretary for defence support to investigate the matter.

Against massive opposition from parliamentary colleagues, the ADF, the AWM, and the bureaucracy, he recommended to the minister and the prime minister that we be formerly and officially recognized.

As a mentor, and one who helped us keep our cool and who was on our side, was Brigadier Neil Weekes, AM, MC. Neil had been a Platoon Commander in Vietnam with 1 RAR, and it was at the Battle at Fire Support Base Balmoral in 1968, that he was awarded the Military Cross.

Soldiers who fought in the 2nd D&E Platoon were being denied help through DVA because there was no record of its existence. Hence they were liars and hence, their claims were dismissed.

You can imagine what that does to a man who has been in combat, is trying to deal with his demons and get his life back under control to be told that you're a liar. It's the potential for suicide at worst, or to a life of mental torment and a miserable existence at best.

It was on 29 May, 2008, 39 years to the day of the battle at Thua Tich that the Australian government gave us official recognition at Parliament House in Canberra.

Two books have been written about the 2nd D&E Platoon: *Ghost Platoon* by Frank Walker (Hachette Australia) and *Anzacs Betrayed* by Don Tate (self-published).

You will see more on the website www.BeatPostTraumaticStressDisorder.com

Chapter 1 – My Story

Part Nine – Army: Do I Stay, Or Do I Go?

The soldier who'd returned

The Kevin Lloyd-Thomas who joined the Army in March 1966 was a very different Kevin from the one who returned from a second tour of duty in Vietnam in November, 1969.

The Kevin in March 1966 was almost a lost soul. It was a Kevin without direction, without ambition, with very little motivation, lacking in self-belief, self-confidence, with very little feeling of any kind of self-worth or self-value. A Kevin who could hardly look you in the eye such was the extent and depth of this lack of self-belief, self-esteem and self-confidence. One who regularly questioned his value and his place in life and who was just drifting without any direction. Why am I even here?

A skinny kid with a face pockmarked with acne, almost always with a scowl on his face, and a head full of negative self-talk. I had been transformed from a cowering failure to a confident young soldier who had seen combat and had seen the best and the worst of what men could do to one another.

I had my 20th and my 21st first birthday in Vietnam, both of them out on operations. I'd been promoted in the field because of my capability, and I'd led men into combat. I'd made decisions under the toughest of combat circumstances, I'd demonstrated my leadership ability, and people knew that they could trust me implicitly. My word was my bond.

The Army had totally transformed me. It was as if I had been reborn. I was happy, and could make decisions about myself and what I wanted to do. I had formed mateships that are still a part of my life to this very day and I was a grown man in every respect of the word at 21 years old.

Vietnam had been an absolute watershed in my life.

Returning home from a war zone

You don't need me to tell you just how euphoric and how good that feeling is the moment you get home from a tour of duty in a combat zone. It's the greatest feeling of freedom because it's finally over.

But what about the anticipation? The build-up in your mind of what it's going to be like to see your loved ones again. Wives, husbands, children? For people like me, the woman of your dreams. Absolutely first and foremost!

For all of the searching of my mind and my memory, I don't recall the time of day or night that I actually landed back in Australia from that second tour, but I do know it was the homecoming of my life.

Sandy took her annual holidays, and as you can imagine, those four weeks were sensational. The 12 months apart was the time we really fell in love.

I also knew that my parents had become very fond of Sandy. In one of my father's very rare letters to me, written while I was at 1 ARU, he wrote something like, "You should marry this girl. She will be very good for you."

How prophetic that was to become.

Chapter 1 – My Story

Back on duty

In mid-January, 1970, I marched into the Third Training Battalion at Singleton.

I drove into the car park at Battalion HQ, taking out my paperwork, walk into Battalion Headquarters, and waited for a brief moment for one of the clerks to come and speak with me. I handed over my documentation and find out I've been posted to E company, an Infantry Corps Training Company. Thank goodness for that and I ask for directions how to get there.

As my paperwork was being processed, the Company Sergeant-Major came out of his office and introduced himself to me. He then took me into the office of the Company Commander to introduce me to him. The Company Commander was Captain Tarmo Rae. You know when you meet somebody for the first time, you just get that intuitive feeling that you either like them or you don't? Well, my initial reaction was that he was an okay bloke.

The next morning was an early start. It was then that I met my Platoon Commander. My intuition said this is not a nice person. I was to find out some time later that my intuition proved correct. He turned out to be a thug and a bully, and that, along with his propensity to bullshit and his smartass attitude, would lead us to clash.

All of my efforts were concentrated on becoming the most professional instructor I could possibly be. I took my role very seriously. Many of these young men would, once they had finished their Infantry training, be sent to Vietnam as reinforcements. I felt it was my duty to ensure that they were trained to the highest standards possible. It was our obligation as their instructors, to give them the greatest benefit possible of our combat experience in Vietnam.

It was my obligation to myself, and to them, to be the very best I could be.

Annual leave

At every opportunity, I couldn't wait to get out of Singleton and the Barracks. I'd drive home to Sydney, staying at my parents' place and spend my weekends with Sandy. If not staying in Sydney, we'd stay with her parents at their weekender at Tumbi Umbi, near The Entrance on the Central Coast. We were madly in love.

It was just prior to Christmas 1970 and I was home on annual leave.

One morning my father dropped and broke his electric razor and asked me to take it into a repair facility in the city.

Coincidentally, next door to the repair facility was a Diamond Traders jewelry store. The repair was able to be done while I waited and it was almost as if some unseen force was drawing me to the jewelry in the display windows. In less than a minute I was inside the store. Within half an hour I bought an engagement ring. Just like that.

Will you marry me?

My best recollection is that my head was spinning, and now, when and how was I going to ask Sandy to marry me?

Sandy would be at my parents place for Sunday lunch.

When I felt the timing was right, I said something to Sandy like, "Could you come into dad's study, there's something I'd like to show you." I shut the door behind us, reached into my pocket, took out the little box, lifted the lid so she could see it, and said, "Will you marry me?" She

Chapter 1 – My Story

threw her arms around my neck, hugging me so tightly while giving me a kiss, then drew back, and said "Yes." Then I slid the ring onto her finger.

"We'd better tell my parents" so that's what we did. They were very happy for us.

Fast forward into 1971

On the 12th of June, 1971, Sandy and I were married. What a beautiful day.

We had our wedding reception at the El Rancho Hotel at Epping. It was a great party, just magical.

At the time, who could possibly have foreseen the future and that my return to the El Rancho would be such a traumatic time?

Do I stay, or do I go?

My decision to leave the Australian Army was a very simple one. They made it very easy for me to say no to them when they asked me to sign on for another three years.

There were three things that made me decide that I was going to leave.

The first?

In a talk to the trainees, my Platoon Commander spruiked a total load of bullshit about Vietnam.

As a professional soldier I was very unhappy about what he said. I approached him to speak about this and we met in his office to speak one on one. I also spoke of his bullying tactics. He had a bad habit when dishing out discipline to have soldiers do pushups and he would use his swagger stick to prod them in the testicles.

He was incensed. "How dare you speak to me like that corporal? Who the fuck do you think you are? What you've just said is insubordination and you're on a charge."

Tarmo Rae the OC persuaded him to drop the charge, but my punishment was being posted to A Company, a Recruit Training company. I became very unhappy.

The second?

A total loss of faith in senior NCOs and senior officers.

After overtaking a military police vehicle on the road between Singleton and well outside the Army camp, they stopped me at least a kilometer inside the area and charged me with speeding. I couldn't believe it. What a joke! That meant I was on a charge and I would have to front the CO.

The day my charge was to be heard I was marched into the CO's office by the RSM.

What a farce. The military police couldn't say what speed I was doing inside the camp. It was based on the fact that they hadn't seen my brake lights come on. The CO dismissed the charge.

It was what happened next that cemented my loss of faith.

The CO had my military record in front of him and asked me why I was posted from E company to A company, a Recruit Training company, so I told him. The RSM exploded. "We'll speak about this outside." "Are we finished, sir?" he said to the CO. "Yes we are" and I'm marched out into the middle of Battalion HQ.

Chapter 1 – My Story

Right in front of everyone, "If your Platoon Commander tells you that black's white then black's white. How dare you question your Platoon Commander?"

I couldn't believe what I was hearing.

"With respect Sir, if my Platoon Commander bullshits to the troops are you telling me I should keep my mouth shut because he's an officer, and I'm an NCO, is that what you're telling me, sir."

The outcome was that I was to do six weekends in a row of Guard Commander. So much for man management and leadership.

The third?

That my Army career had been stopped dead in its tracks by a Battalion Commander in whom I had lost faith because of his view of how one should conduct one's self as an NCO, and as someone aspiring to be an officer.

Earlier I said that I had made it my obligation to myself to be the best instructor I could be.

I decided I wanted to become an Officer. I felt I'd be a very good one because of my combat experience, my experience as an instructor, and I wanted to make the Army my career. I put myself through school at night to get the required standard of education.

To be accepted into the Officer Cadet School at Portsea (OCS) and as one coming from the ranks, my application would need the approval of the Commandant of Infantry, and the Commandant of OCS, which I duly received. The final approval required would be from my Commanding Officer.

The outcome was this; now I was in front of the Colonel again, and in front of him was my Army record of service.

"Corporal Lloyd-Thomas, I know this must mean a lot to you, you've obviously worked hard to achieve this, and I note that you have both other approvals. However, I will not approve this application."

It was like a punch in the guts.

"Why not sir?" I asked. Then then there was a silence that seemed to last for minutes, but it must have been for only a few seconds.

"Because corporal, I don't believe you would be socially acceptable as an officer. You have a bad habit of speaking out of turn and don't know when to keep your opinions to yourself. You don't have the discipline to be an effective officer, and you would continually put your superior officers offside."

What was he saying? This was just his subjective opinion.

"Permission to speak sir?" I asked. He nodded.

"I find it very difficult to accept that you see me as being socially unacceptable, whatever that means. What about my capability as a soldier, as an instructor, what about my combat experience and leadership capability, what about what trainees have written and said about me to both of my Company Commanders? Doesn't any of that count, sir?"

"Corporal, I've said all I'm going to say. Your application is not approved. March out."

To say that I was devastated would be an understatement. But there it was, I was not going to be an Officer in the Australian Army.

Chapter 1 – My Story

Should I Go, Or Should I Stay?

That's when I made the decision I was going to get out. That's when I started to plan my life after the Army.

Where to next and what to do? What did I do to prepare myself for the day I left the Army?

First, I started to ask questions of my father and his business colleagues. Almost without exception, I was advised to get a commercial qualification, and the most common directions that I was advised to go in was in sales and marketing. This meant more study at night, so I enrolled in a Marketing Certificate course with International Correspondence Schools.

It was hard work, but I sat the final exam, and got the Certificate.

One of the key questions I faced is how do I relate my military skills to the civilian world, particularly having been an Infantry soldier?

What skills did I have that a prospective employer could relate to? What benefit could they be to that prospective employer? How do I sell those benefits to them so they employ me, instead of a civilian candidate, because of their value to the employer, skills most civilians don't have?

Apart from specific trade skills, what skills do we have in common that are marketable and have value? Skills we get at an early age because we've been in the military?

Here are some of them:

- Physical discipline
- Mental discipline
- Personal discipline
- Man management
- Time management
- Communication skills
- Leadership skills
- Decision making
- Taking action
- Risk management
- Teamwork
- Organization skills
- Adaptability

What else do you do that will separate you from your civilian counterparts, so that an employer can see very easily and quickly that you really have done your homework?

You know what their business is about, you know who their customers are, you know who their competitors are, you know about the latest technology that may affect their business, either good or bad, and what else do you know?

There's more about this in Chapter 8, The Five Step Life Plan.

Leaving The Army

I'll give you a specific illustration below of the value of being prepared. This is exactly the way it happened, but first, the day finally arrived, the day I'd been preparing for.

Chapter 1 – My Story

Six weeks short of my 24th birthday, on the 14 March, 1972, I took my discharge from the Army. Initially, after being discharged I joined the AMP Society as an insurance salesman. My brother Nigel, after his two years of National Service had joined AMP and was doing very well. He persuaded me that if he could then I could, so that's what I did.

It took me about nine months to realize that this was not for me. I really struggled with it, wrote very few policies, and felt I was continually under pressure, so I started to look around for another opportunity.

I saw an advertisement in the paper placed by J Blackwood & Son Limited, seeking applicants for its Management Trainee Program. When I read through the advertisement and the qualifications and experience they were seeking, there were some that I didn't have, in particular the level of formal education.

I applied anyway, and some days later I received a letter asking me to call them to arrange a time for an interview.

This is what's important about doing your homework, and about thinking outside the square.

The advice given to me by a next door neighbor was that I go to the Sydney Stock Exchange to get a copy of that company's annual report to find out as much as I could about them and their competitors, so that's what I did.

The day of the interview came around, and it was with the General Manager, Dick Hanlon. After a few minutes of asking me some brief questions about being in the Army and how I was finding things now, he asked me this question: "Apart from the fact that Blackwood's sells bolts and nuts, what else do you know about the company?"

73

I was able to describe the company's transition from being a family company to being a public company listed on the stock exchange, their current share price, their market capitalization, the dividend paid to shareholders. I'd seen a copy of their Industrial Catalogue at the Stock Exchange Library. I was able to describe the range of products that they sold, their top ten customers, some of the major suppliers, and who were their biggest competitors.

Why should they employ me, and if I were to become one of their management trainees, what benefit would I bring to the company?

The end result was that I got a start on the company's first management trainee program.

I can say unequivocally to this day, that the J Blackwood and Son Limited I was with for 13 years was the best company I have ever worked for. It was one of Australia's most innovative and creative industrial distribution businesses at that time.

As a management trainee I started off in the warehouse as a storeman and packer to learn about the products and how the warehouse operation worked. How far you went in the company from there was entirely up to you.

Over a period of 13 years, I went through telephone sales, being a sales representative, to becoming the companies first pricing and contracts manager, to then being the Head Office inventory controller.

I was headhunted by White International to become its first Operations Manager, and it was from there, when Blackwood's went into the market for a new computer system, that I was approached by Mike and ABC Systems in 1985.

You already know what happened from there.

CHAPTER 2

WHAT WAS THE RESULT?

CHAPTER 2
– WHAT WAS THE RESULT?

It's the afternoon of Monday, the 24th of January 1994, after leaving ABC and I'm now unemployed. It's now time to get on with the rest of my life.

It was the start of what was to become a nightmare journey for me but I didn't know it at the time. Was I in for a shock or what?

If you told me then that it would be almost three years before I found a full-time job I would've told you that you must be off with the pixies at the bottom of the garden. What were you drinking? What were you sniffing? What sort of weed were you on?

Looking for a job

It was time to think outside the square to the greatest degree possible.

I listed every single solitary company I could think of who I knew that I could approach for work. I then went through the Yellow Pages phone directory, again listing every single company that could be a candidate for my services, and it was across every industry I could think of.

I made a very specific point of phoning every target company to find out to whom I should address a letter. I wrote literally hundreds of letters. I'd put a cover letter with my resume and relate how my skills would be of relevance, value and benefit, very specifically, to their particular business.

Chapter 2 – What Was The Result?

I didn't keep an exact count of the number of letters I wrote but it was in excess of 350. It was also disheartening that less than 30 of those companies I contacted actually wrote back to say 'thanks but no thanks.'

What was so disheartening too was that even follow-up phone calls to the specific people to whom I had written, less than 20 of those people actually paid the courtesy of returning a follow-up phone call.

Not one door opened, not a single one.

Disappointment after disappointment

Then there are the 476 job applications directly to companies, and through professional consultants.

In all of the time I was searching for employment, I got shortlisted twice and got one final interview. That role, as the General Manager of a company in the industrial insulation business was given to another candidate, but I'll never forget the circumstances. It's worth relating briefly for this book because it's about humanity, decency, and the essence of integrity and character, traits which are missing, and on an international basis, from many of our CEO's, boards of directors, and political and religious leaders, if you can call some of them that.

I knew the company from my days at Blackwood's. It had been a family company and had been bought by a business investor.

I had two preliminary interviews and got a call from the owner of the business asking me to attend a final interview. I was pretty excited about this because I knew I could steer this company to greater and more profitable success.

The final interview went very well and I was confident this could finally be where I would end up and working in a business I knew I could grow.

A couple of days later I got a phone call from the owner asking me to meet with him again at his home in Rose Bay. We sat down in his study which was a big comfortable room full of antique furniture and with a massive bay window which gave a stunning view of the ocean.

"Kevin" he said, "I don't have good news for you and I'm finding it very difficult to tell you this. You're the ideal candidate for this role and I know you would be very good for this business, but I'm going to give the role to another gentleman who desperately needs it."

I could see he was finding it very difficult to speak. As he spoke his eyes would frequently leave mine and I could see and tell he was very close to tears. "This man has been out of work for almost as long as you have, but unlike you, he has three very young children and that's why I am giving him the job. He's just so desperate and I feel that I must help him."

Almost word for word he said: "Right now Kevin, I don't like myself as a good person today, but I must do what my heart tells me and I hope you'll forgive me for that." The tears started to run down his face.

I have never been in a situation like that before. Here was a man obviously very wealthy, and very successful with tears running down his face telling me he was sorry he couldn't give me a job because he had to give it to someone else less fortunate than me.

Was I disappointed? You bet I was, but did I understand? Yes I did. I realized how difficult it must have been for him to have me come into his home to tell me what he had just told me. I don't know whether he's still on the planet, but what I can say is that he is one of the most impressive men I've ever met and I wish I could remember his name.

That man had real ethics and real integrity. He had real character and real compassion, all of the qualities I admire in a man or a woman.

As I drove away I had very mixed emotions. I was still unemployed and I was almost at the end of my tether, but by the same token, I was just so impressed by the experience I had just had.

Going begging for a job

The next morning in sheer desperation I rang Peter Fay, who was now the managing director at Blackwood's. When I had left almost 13 years before, Peter was the National Sales Manager. I asked him if he would be able to give me some time to see if there might be an opportunity for me at Blackwood's.

I explained my situation and yes he would meet with me the next day at two-thirty in the afternoon. I remember it very clearly.

Where to start? So I just blurted it out. "I'm begging for a job, Peter. I'll start right at the bottom if I have to and work my way back on merit just like everyone else. Telephone sales, department sales, something, anything, I'll do whatever it takes."

I could hardly control my emotions as I told Peter of my experience over the last almost three years. Almost verbatim, "Kev, we now have a policy where we don't rehire former employees and no matter how much I'd love to make an exception for you I can't."

My heart sank at those words.

While I was still at Blackwood's, the company had been taken over by Howard Smith Industries, who had also taken over the national BBC Hardware group. Peter told me he was on the board of BBC and he was meeting the next day with Ian Tsicalas, now Managing Director of BBC and Deputy Managing Director of Howard Smith. I knew Ian very well and I'd call him a friend at that time, as he is still to this day. Peter would give him my resume, make him aware of our discussion and ask if there might be any openings or opportunities for me at BBC.

Nothing happening?

Almost two weeks later the phone rang at about 7:30 am in the morning. It was Ian.

"Have you got anything on today Kev?" he asked. "No I don't" I said. "Could you be at my office at Epping at 11:30 this morning?" "Absolutely, Ian."

I can tell you my heart was racing. Could this be the start of a long-term opportunity for me at BBC? Fingers crossed. It could be, but nothing like I expected. Another chapter in my life was about to unfold.

In that meeting Ian made me aware that BBC had taken over another hardware group and the role he saw for me was to integrate the pricing structure of that group into the BBC structure. It would be a six-month contract and he was giving it to me.

He made me aware that he didn't want to give me any false hopes, he couldn't create a job for me as much as he would like to, but if something came up that made me the ideal candidate, the role would be mine.

Chapter 2 – What Was The Result?

Six months later, the task is complete, with the exception of one last supplier and in a discussion with Ian, there's no opening for me at BBC, so I'm now back looking for employment, once the last little bit is done.

If I thought the last three years were a rollercoaster ride I had another one coming, it would become more intense, and the downward spiral would increase at an ever more rapid rate.

A stroke of luck from left-field driven by a former client at ABC. Whoopee!

I made a phone call to the last company on my list, JUB International, a supplier to BBC and Blackwood's as well. I knew the company and its product ranges.

The person best able to help me with the information I needed was the New South Wales State Manager, Jill Jones. By sheer coincidence, while I was at ABC systems she had been the General Manager of Moore's Merchants, and I had sold them a complete computer hardware and software package.

The timing couldn't have been better. Jill made me aware she had resigned and would be leaving the following Friday, and I told her that JUB was the last company on the list at BBC and my contract was finished. You are the perfect candidate for my job, Kevin.

We agreed I would drop a copy of my resume to her first thing next morning, she would fax it to her Managing Director, tell him about me and set up an interview, and that's what happened.

A week later I was the new State Manager.

At JUB, a series of circumstances arose, most of which were beyond my control. Being forced to downsize the operation, to lay off staff, losing massive slabs of business from our biggest customers like Blackwood's and BBC because we could no longer compete on price, but it was me who had to deal with them.

At the time I paid little or no attention to what was happening in my mind, dismissing the fits of anger, the berating of myself for accepting criticism with no argument when I couldn't recover the lost business, such was my loss of confidence in myself. I just accepted it and made the decision to leave before I was pushed out the door.

For some reason, over a 48-hour period, or even less, I could go from the Kevin on the outside, to the Kevin on the inside.

The Kevin on the outside was confident, creative, great at winning people's confidence, able to enthuse and motivate people.

Then there was the Kevin on the inside. Paralyzed to the core with fear, paralyzed with self-doubt, with an intense fear of failure, complete loss of self-belief, no shred of self-worth, a useless failure who would never amount to anything, berating himself, and not just with the voice in his head, but also out loud. "What the fuck is wrong with you, you fucking idiot? What the fuck is stopping you?"

After leaving JUB, I'd gone into real estate sales. Fired from one, and about to be fired from the next one. The same thing happened - the massive highs and almost bottomless lows. My saviour was the number of referrals I gave to a mortgage broker I worked with. I wouldn't show property to anyone if we didn't have their finance in place, and she got anywhere between five and 30 referrals a month from me.

Chapter 2 – What Was The Result?

A new year and a new challenge.

I was invited to a Christmas function at the mortgage brokers office in Crow's Nest, and it was at that function I met the two owners of the business, Peter Wesley and Glenn Maynard.

They were aware that I was the person who gave them a substantial volume of referrals.

Early in the New Year, Glenn asked me to come and have a cup of coffee to talk about a couple of ideas. It was also the time he asked me if I would consider coming to work for them, and my answer was yes. I was able to resign from real estate sales without being fired.

It all started wonderfully, but a few months later, the Kevin on the inside was back again.

Two of the guys were playing with a tennis ball, throwing it to one another almost the entire length of the office. One of them was almost behind me when the ball was thrown quite forcibly to him. He was never going to catch it and it smashed into the back of my computer screen. Instantly I dropped to the floor. An absolutely instantaneous reflex reaction. "What the fuck was that?"

There's that conditioning again

He apologized profusely. The whole office came to a standstill because of the noise of the ball hitting the computer screen, me dropping to the floor then screaming out, and my colleague apologizing for what happened.

I was so shaken, so angry, so enraged I had to leave the office. I was shaking almost uncontrollably as I walked down the stairs and out of the office. "What the fuck is happening to me?" I asked myself as I walked down the street.

I felt physically sick, there was a knot of fear in my guts, my breath was coming in shallow gasps, my shoulders started to heave as my guts churned over and I vomited violently into the gutter, then burst into tears, shaking uncontrollably. "Faaaark! I can't do this anymore, I just can't." I muttered out loud as I leant against a tree holding my head in my hands.

A lady passing by stopped and asked me "Are you okay?" "Yeah, I'm fine but it's just been a tough day. It'll sort itself out, but thanks for asking. I really appreciate it."

That was the incident which finally made me recognize I needed help. I was falling apart. I felt totally helpless, almost without hope. My life was disintegrating right in front of me and there was fuck all I could do about it, and finally, finally, I knew it.

I went back to the office, packed up my things and headed for home. I was just completely and utterly drained. I made a phone call, then went home via the pub. I needed some of those little white pills. That evening in a discussion with Sandy and her dad, I asked if they thought I should go and see a psychiatrist and ask for help.

They both agreed I should, and that's when I made the decision. I was heading for the black abyss at an accelerating rate, and it had finally been rammed home to me.

CHAPTER 3

WAKING UP TO THE PROBLEM

CHAPTER 3
– WAKING UP TO THE PROBLEM

On Monday morning I rang my GP and asked if I could see him urgently to which he agreed. I told him what happened. The meltdown in the street. The realization I needed help. The discussion with Sandy and her father Ted and that I wanted to see a psychiatrist, one who was familiar with the military.

He gave me a referral and I went straight home to set up an appointment.

I rang the office of Donald Phillips (not his real name). I explained to the receptionist that I was in trouble and needed to see him as quickly as possible and made an appointment. The earliest I could get in to see him was the following week.

In going to see Donald, I was actually asking for help for a second time.

What was it that had occurred sometime in the past, and it was years in the past, that made this happen? What was it about ***the first time I'd asked for help?***

Denial

Denial, that's what it was – it was ending up pretending it wasn't there, or that it would go away.

DENIAL – This is **THE single biggest problem** about PTSD and asking for help. It is, by far and away, ***the*** biggest hurdle to be overcome!

Chapter 3 – Waking Up To The Problem

The other major hurdle *is fear itself*, and *fear of the stigma that can come with it*, and in far too many cases, *actually does*. What will my mates think of me? What will my boss think of me? What about my career?

When you get yourself to the point where this hurdle is overcome, when you stop listening to this bullshit story we keep telling ourselves about "There's nothing wrong with me," then you'll be on your way.

It's about admitting to yourself that you do have a problem, accepting it then asking for help. You can now do that, and no one else needs to know. We'll talk more about this later.

Is this a "Me too" moment?

I'd like a $20 bill for every time I told myself there's nothing wrong with me, or made an excuse for the way I was behaving, the way I was thinking, or the way I felt. I'd have a bucket load of money, and it would be in the thousands!

But that's what denial is all about

The truth can be staring you in the face, and deep, deep down, you know it's the truth, but still you deny it. There's nothing wrong with me, there's nothing wrong with me, but deep down in the place I call my Sanctum Santorum, the place where only I know the truth, and the real truth, I knew it was bullshit.

What about you? A *"Me too" moment?*

To put it bluntly, I'd been bullshitting myself for years.

Why was I doing this to myself? The truth is, deep down in my subconscious mind, I knew I had a problem, but my conscious mind kept telling me that there was nothing wrong. I'd get over it, and apart from that, I wasn't a bludger or a shirker, it was only those piss-weak bastards who said they had a problem.

Another "Me too" moment?

From what I've been able to determine through research, speaking with many mental health professionals, and in the discussion with many other veterans and serving men and women, being in denial that you do in fact have a problem is probably the single most common factor in creating an even bigger issue in the future.

It makes a massive contribution to a broadening of symptoms, greater potential personal damage, far greater damage to relationships, particularly to wives and children, and making it even harder to make that decision that's in your own best interests.

Taking a step back in time – do I have a problem?

On Anzac Day in 1993, and while still at ABC systems, I was having a conversation with Jock Kennedy who had been our platoon medic on my first tour of Vietnam. I was telling Jock about the almost relentless pressure at ABC Systems, the highs and lows I was experiencing, and we were talking about PTSD and what had happened to a couple of our mates.

As a result of this without saying anything to anyone I went to see the Vietnam Veterans Federation and asked them to get me in touch with a psychiatrist because I was having a few problems. Within two weeks, for

Chapter 3 – Waking Up To The Problem

the first time in my life, I went to see a psychiatrist. The outcome of that was he told me I had PTSD, I should apply for a TPI pension through DVA, and he gave me a prescription for the antidepressant, Zoloft.

I point-blank refused to apply for a TPI because I said I was not a bludger. I didn't need a TPI, I just needed help, so for three or four months I saw the psychiatrist every two or three weeks, then I stopped.

The long-term outcome of this was I would get my prescription for Zoloft renewed without any problems.

You know the story of that, and what happened from there.

ABC Systems: The almost 3 year rollercoaster ride of unemployment, four different employers, the same rollercoaster. Was it at an end?

CHAPTER 4

ASKING FOR HELP

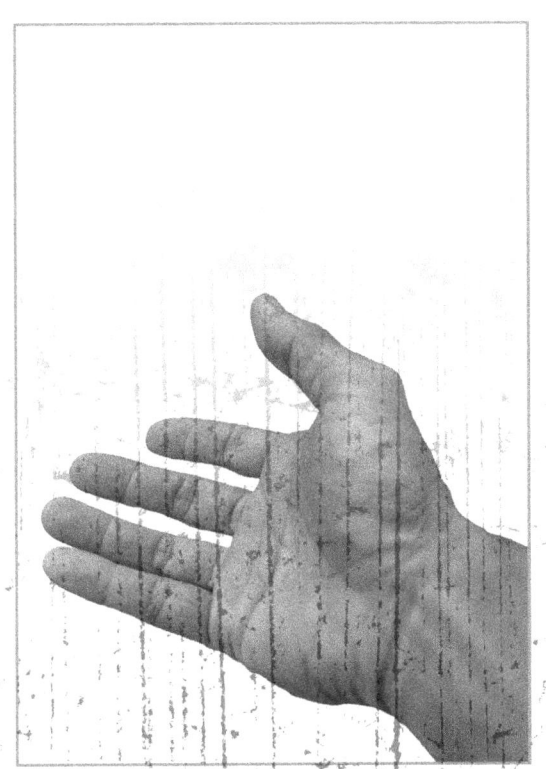

CHAPTER 4
– ASKING FOR HELP

It was late 2001 when I first went to see Donald Phillips.

His first question to me was to ask if I'd sought help before.

"Yes I have" I said. I briefly described what was happening over most of 1993 at ABC Systems, including the events surrounding the state of mind I was in when I decided to go to the Vietnam Veterans Association around March or April, 1993 as best I could recall the timing.

I described the sequence of events that lead to the doctor telling me I had PTSD, prescribing Zoloft to me, and that I should apply for a TPI. I told him about my reaction to that, that there was no way I'd apply for a TPI, because no one was going to call me a bludger or a shirker. I wasn't going to be one of those men who took a TPI instead of dealing with the problem.

When I said that I noticed Donald close his eyes and almost imperceptibly, shake his head from side to side. I couldn't understand why he would do that until he said something like, "I just hear this so often and it's all about the stigma of asking for help, so okay, Kevin, what happened after that?"

We spoke of everything that happened over the intervening years until right now, with me sitting in front of him knowing I need help.

I told Donald that for nearly eight years I felt I'd been living in an 'In Between' world.

Chapter 4 – Asking For Help

Over the next few weeks we discussed all aspects of this in almost minute details as Donald stepped me through all of my experiences, all the while asking me what I thought and how I felt about each incident. It was so hard as I relived all that I'd gone through and in the most minute details as Donald probed my memory, my mind, and in my feelings and reflections.

What Happened Next?

At the end of one of our sessions, the next question from Donald took me by surprise. "How do you and Sandy stand financially?" "We're quite okay but why do you ask?" Donald replied, "If you stopped work, would the two of you be able to live reasonably well?" "Yes, we would" I said.

"From what we've discussed over the last several weeks Kevin", he said, "My diagnosis is that you have chronic PTSD coupled with substance, alcohol and tobacco abuse. My recommendation is that you immediately apply for a TPI. We can fill out the application form now and I'll attach all of the supporting information required and get it to DVA."

"Let's do it" I said, and I felt as if a 50-ton block had been lifted from my shoulders.

DVA, 19th March, 2002 – then came the verdict

It was almost six weeks to the day that I got a letter from DVA advising they had accepted the claim submitted by Donald on my behalf and I now had TPI status with them.

As you can imagine there was the bureaucratic part of it and the information I would need to provide them with to get everything finalized, but the most important part was I could let Glenn know that my TPI had come through and that I would be resigning from the Mortgage Store.

Sandy's reaction was ecstatic. "This is just wonderful. How do you feel about it?"

"It's like the world has been lifted from my shoulders", I said.

"I can finally see a way ahead, a far less stressful life without the relentless pressure of having to perform, carrying the weight of what happened to me and how do I turn it around. The damage it's done to our relationship. How it almost drove us apart. I just didn't realize how much I was hurting you, what I was doing to you, how I was driving a wedge into our marriage, how I was only thinking of myself, and I'm so sorry for that."

Ten years ago, if you told me then that I'd be in this position now, I would've said you must be off with the pixies. What have you been smoking? What have you been sniffing? What are you shooting into your arm?

But here we were. I'd finally asked for help, there was just such a feeling of relief. It's finally happened. I can free up my mind, I can get away from the torture of nightmares, panic attacks, night sweats, the anger, just the whole fucking mess of what my life has been like for eight years or more. Just blessed relief.

Could this be a *"Me too moment"* for you? Seriously?

If you haven't asked for help yet, what about considering what you've just read? Maybe a *'parachute moment?'* Could it be the best thing you

Chapter 4 – Asking For Help

could do for yourself and for your family – you, and they, could come out winners. Nothing surer! What do you think?

Day one of mental freedom

The Friday afternoon I walked out of the Mortgage Store for the last time was a bit emotional too. I realized my life had just changed. It would be a whole new paradigm and I didn't know quite what to expect. What I did know was that I now had to do whatever it takes to put my demons at rest.

Little did I know or suspect what was to happen over the next few months.

Starting the slide downhill – again

It was unnoticeable at first but started to gather momentum when people started to ask me what I did for a living. It became a bit of a dilemma, and because of what had happened at that program, I became embarrassed and ashamed to tell people I was on a TPI, so I said I had retired. Then the more stories I heard about men putting in claims for TPI who had never been near any action of any sort, the angrier I got about it and the more embarrassed and more ashamed I got too.

I started to feel guilty about my situation and how I'd let myself get there, and I started to mentally and verbally bash myself again. What a failure I was. Just look at me, yeah, just look at me. I'm 54 years old. I'm a complete fucking failure, I'm on a fucking pension, and I can't work. What a bloody drongo. What must people think of me, I started to wonder.

Also, almost unnoticeably at first, I was starting to drink earlier and earlier in the day, I was staying up late at night more and more frequently, sleeping less and less, and more and more frequently getting irritable and angry.

It came to a head one weekend when Sandy told me she was unhappy and wanted to have a serious discussion about how she felt with a number of things in our relationship and marriage, and in our day to day lives.

When I reflect back and think about it now, I can see now how I made life for her one of purgatory and no wonder she was unhappy.

I had become extremely selfish, it was always about me, it was almost as if I just did as I pleased with no consideration for her, what she might think, how she might feel, and the impact my attitude and behavior was having on her.

But I'd never thought about any of those things at the time. I just did what I did.

The first thing was she was getting more and more unhappy about was my drinking. It was getting to a point where I was drinking heavily each night. Sandy enjoyed a glass of wine with dinner and would have one or two glasses, maybe three every now and then. But for me, I'd already started drinking before she got home from work and by 9.30 or 10 o'clock at night I was well and truly drunk.

Another "Me too" moment?

She told me she was getting sick and tired of my erratic behavior, and with hindsight I can now see it. One day I'm fine, I'm happy, she's happy

Chapter 4 – Asking For Help

and everything is okay. Then something happens and I get angry and start shouting. Maybe I'm laying down the law, maybe I'm disagreeing with something she has said or done.

She's tired of my temper tantrums. Something goes wrong with something I'm doing, or she's doing and I lose my temper. I'm always right, she's always wrong.

Then I get sullen and won't even speak.

Then it's all over and I'm back to normal. But it's not normal. There's always a next time, and there always was, and it wasn't just every pancake day.

And always again, with hindsight, it must have been terrible for her, and what I inflicted on her because of what was happening in my head, and, as always, at the time, I could justify it in my own mind.

The beginning of the end

We'd also started to argue about money, and most particularly what was happening in my Super Fund.

Sandy had never been happy about my stock market dealings, and wanted us to get back into the property market.

Exactly how it happened I'm not sure of, but one day we sat down to thrash this out. I have a recollection of saying something like, "Okay let's start looking at property. Let's look at the idea of cashing in the shares or most of them and buying property. We own this place and the unit and between them they are worth a lot of money. We can use the equity in both properties and use it to fund other properties. If we're smart we'll have it positively geared so it completely pays for itself."

We agreed to start exploring the property market to see what was around and what we could do.

The end

One night we had a massive argument about the whole thing. It got pretty nasty and 99% from me. I accused her of always standing in my way, because she was so conservative and in my opinion was getting worse. I hurled at her "You've always held us back because you're so bloody conservative and it will never change." It just went on and on as I put the blame on her for virtually everything that had happened to me, and was happening to us. If this, if that, if anything. It's all your fault.

My erratic behavior, my drinking, angry outbursts, fits of temper and general demeanor continued and put even more strain on our marriage after that, and at a point Sandy could no longer tolerate it.

One night after dinner she said she'd had enough and felt we should separate for a while and see if we still wanted to stay together. My immediate reaction was no way, we're not separating. We'll just have to try and sort it out.

In my mind, I mulled over it night after night, day after day, agonising over what to do.

After dinner one night, that's when I told her. "I've been thinking this over for the last two weeks after you said you felt we should separate for a while, and now I agree. You have to do what you want to do your way,

Chapter 4 – Asking For Help

and I've made the decision I want to go my own way. That way we're both going to be happy and there'll be no arguments or recriminations later."

Sandy was taken aback a bit, then said yes, she agreed we'd both be unhappy, and there's no point in living that way.

We agreed we'd sell the house, split everything 50-50, I would buy her out of the Balmain property which would become my home, she would stay with her parents until she found somewhere else to live, and that was the end of our marriage.

In August 2003, we were going our own separate ways.

Maybe a "Me too" moment for you?

Finality – 18th August, 2003

The removalists arrived, and within five or six hours the house was emptied.

Our cars were parked in the street. We stood on the nature strip and looked down at the house we'd lived in for 17 years and now it was just an empty shell. A home that had been, but was no longer.

We gave each other a hug and wished each other well then got into our cars.

Sandy went in one direction, and I went in another.

Another "Me too" moment? Perhaps?

A clean slate

Another chapter of my life had closed and another one was opening up.

I felt I was starting the next chapter of my life with an absolutely clean slate.

Here I am. I own a waterfront apartment at Balmain with views over Sydney Harbour. I have money in the bank. I've got a superfund which I manage and for income I have my TPI and service pension.

From any perspective you'd say I was in a pretty comfortable position, and I was.

A short time after I'd stopped work, I went to the Sydney Boat Show at Darling Harbour. Very particularly I was looking for sailing schools that would be promoting themselves at the show.

Learning to sail was something I'd always wanted to do, but had never taken the time or made the time to turn it into a reality, and here was my opportunity.

It was there that I found the Allsail Sailing School based at Church Point on Pittwater. They had a fleet of eight or ten J/24 keelboats as sail training boats, and an Adams 44 named *Kickatinalong* because it was made out of aluminium. This was also used for sail training but its main use was for offshore racing.

I'd promised myself that if I ever took up sailing and had the opportunity to do the Sydney to Hobart Yacht Race, then I'd do it. If I only ever did it once that would be okay. Forever I could say that I've done one and that would be pretty special.

Chapter 4 – Asking For Help

Learning to sail was one of the best things I've ever done for myself. When I reflect back if I'd known about the joys of sailing when I left the Army, I would have tried to find a way to get into sailing as a way of earning an income.

I wasn't to know it at the time, but it was sailing, and in a curious way, that saved me from taking my own life, and you'll learn more about that at the end of the next chapter.

I can say now, that the greatest therapy I've ever discovered for myself is sailing.

I know that the time I'm at total and utter at peace with myself is when I am out on the ocean. Whether it's racing or not, that's *the time when I'm at peace both within and without.*

Sailing has a direct correlation with the military. To be able to sail safely out on the ocean requires individual skills, and it requires teamwork. Everyone in the crew has a job to do, everyone is reliant on everyone else, implicit trust is required, and when the shit hits the fan you know that your teammate has your back, and they know you have theirs.

At the end of 2003, I was in a good place. You'd certainly think so, but what a rollercoaster ride was to come which was to slam me not once, not twice, but thrice. Whammo!

Then 2004 was a pretty good year. The superfund was doing very well, I was sailing three or four days a week and I was feeling bullet-proof. I did my first Sydney to Hobart Yacht Race, and although we had to pull out late in the race with gear failure, it was one hell of an experience and I was looking forward to 2005 as a very good year

The year that started pretty well, but there was a major setback with the totally unexpected liquidation of Heritage fine wines where I'd made a substantial investment in collectable wines for sale into the American and Chinese markets. The net result was I got three bottles of the 53 bottles of Grange Hermitage I thought I owned, and could only recover $5000 of the other $53,000 I had invested. Bugger! $71,000 down the toilet.

What capped off the year for me was to finish that years Sydney to Hobart Yacht Race. Just magical. I got pretty emotional within myself when we tied up at Constitution Dock in Hobart at about 5.30 in the morning. I'd actually finished a Sydney–Hobart. Bloody awesome. The highlight of the race was hitting 28 knots sailing downwind across Storm Bay.

In 2005, I'd also decided to take a $150,000 mortgage against my unit to put into the superfund to accelerate its ability to invest more widely.

In 2006, I met my partner, Irene. That was pretty special. Another good year you might say, but a big disappointment in having our 2006 entry in the Hobart race disallowed on Christmas Eve due to a technicality. Two naval architects arguing over calculating the 'righting moment' of the boat. It was 1 degree in 116 degrees. Bugger.

Little by little, things started to unravel. My behavior was becoming more and more erratic and I was heading back down the path of destruction again. I was up to 200mg a day on Zoloft, and drinking more. On the days I wasn't sailing I was getting lazier and lazier and spending less time on my Super Fund.

The fiasco of the StockMaster Systems in 2007 was another financial

Chapter 4 – Asking For Help

blow. Instead of it being floated on the stock market, without warning, it was put into liquidation. Another $50,000 gone.

The feature of the next five years was the Global Financial Crisis which started in the US in 2008 and still has its ramifications today.

The GFC was my undoing. It was the catalyst of a spiral down into the blackest place I'd ever been.

It was a place where I was living in a haze of anger, rage, irrationality, and what you could almost describe as a world of stupor. Such was the state of my mind that I was incapable of rational thinking, I was incapable of making complex decisions. I just drifted through the days and nights bashing myself as I went through this rollercoaster of massive lows, the odd little bit of high before I started bashing the shit out of myself again.

I was constantly berating myself, telling myself what a failure and a fool I was. How the fuck had I let it get to this? I was blaming myself for everything that had happened, but at the same time I was blaming others as well. I was so angry about so many of the stories like Allco Finance, Babcock and Brown, ABC Learning, and many other companies I'd invested in that had gone to the wall. Companies I'd invested in where the directors kept their millions but people like me were financially crushed.

The aftermath of it all was being forced to close my self-managed superfund in March 2011. The superfund was gone, I'd lost over $350,000, and I owed the bank $80,000.

CHAPTER 5

THE ROLLERCOASTER

CHAPTER 5
– THE ROLLERCOASTER

Mind games – sound familiar?

It was almost as if my mind had decided to show me who was the boss. "It's not you Kevin on the outside who's the boss here" it said. "It's me, Kevin on the inside who's the boss. I'm your mind Kevin, and I'm in control of everything that happens to you. You want some more bad shit? I'll find it for you mate, and I'm bloody good at it too. When would you like me to start?"

I had hit rock bottom. I was about to turn 63 and it was as if I had nothing. All I had was a DVA pension and a debt to the bank.

I went spiralling out of control. Drinking heavily every day, and with that, back came the nightmares, the panic attacks, the sleepless nights of tossing and turning, waking up in the early hours of the morning lying in a sea of perspiration that soaked the bedsheets, and beating the shit out of myself.

The nightmares came back with such vengeance there was many a night where I'd wake up, having flung myself out of bed as the Viet Cong soldier with the mouth full of gold teeth, stepping over the log on the track as he bore down on me to try and kill me. The Viet Cong girl with her jaw hanging off below her ear, and her face and half of her neck shot away, screaming at me I kill you, I kill you pointing her AK-47 at me.

Then there's my father with his face no more than an inch from mine.

Chapter 5 – The Rollercoaster

It's contorted with rage as he bellows and screams at me, "You good for nothing jackanapes, you fucking waster, you failure, you piece of nothing, you no good piece of shit, you'll never amount to anything," and I can feel his spittle landing on my face such is the vehemence and ferocity of his verbal attack.

Forty-eight hours of sheer torture

I was in the deepest and darkest of places I had ever been in my life. My daily existence was one of alcohol and self-pity, mercilessly, both out loud, and in my mind, constantly and almost without let up, berating myself as 'Kevin on the inside' tore into me.

"You useless idiot, you fucking fool, why didn't you stop the stupidity earlier, why the fuck didn't you shut the super fund down while you still had some money? What difference would it have made?"

It went on and on. Day after day, night after night. Another nightmare would attack me and I'd lie in bed wide awake for hour after hour, gripped with fear, as I smashed into myself again in the darkness.

"Why don't you just end it all said Kevin on the inside? Quick and simple and nothing will matter anymore. You won't have to worry about a thing. No more nightmares, no more panic attacks, and you won't have to beat the shit out of yourself any more. Just peace."

It started to gnaw away at me as I got to a point of sheer physical and mental exhaustion. The more I thought of it the more it became an option in my mind. Such was the depth of my depression, the self-pity, the abhorrence of myself, and my self-loathing that it was almost as if I was floating in a vacuum and so it became real.

Such was the delicacy of my mental state that I was drifting in a haze of alcohol and self-pity, totally incapable of rational thought, and it was in this other world that I had descended into that I decided to end it all. I rationalized that there was nothing left to live for, there was no meaning left in life for me, I was just a waste of space.

I got in my car and drove south. As I drove, I was totally and utterly oblivious to everything that was going on around me. It was like I was driving in a bubble of nothingness and everything was on autopilot, even the car.

I turned off the freeway onto a local road, then off that road onto a bush track. Having been there before I knew there was a car park at the end which overlooked a cliff. I knew there was a fire trail that led to another part of the cliff face because I'd walked down it, and I knew that once I was off the track, there would be nothing in the way to stop me from taking myself to a better place, so I carefully drove down it and stopped the car about 15 m from the cliff face.

Through the windscreen I could see the ocean. From the horizon back to the cliff edge it looked a little bit like a very deep saucer with trees on the right and trees on the left and the saucer of ocean in the middle.

In my world of nothingness, I put the car into drive, held the hand brake on in my left hand, ready to drop it, and put my foot to the floor.

Once I let that brake go, there would be no way I could stop the car. I knew that. Deep, deep, deep, breaths.

As I took the next deep breath, ready to let the brake go and hurtle over the cliff, a yacht came into view heading north.

It was as if an unseen fist punched me in the guts.

Chapter 5 – The Rollercoaster

I watched mesmerized as the yacht moved across the water.

My breath exploded out of me as the unseen hand of the fist that had punched me in the guts took hold of my hand, put the hand brake on, put the gear shift into park, then tapped me on the knee, and Kevin on the inside said, "take your foot off the throttle mate."

As the tears rolled down my face, and my body heaved and shook almost uncontrollably, I thought what would Irene think, what would this do to her? She'd taken so much shit from me, but had given me so much, like a gift. What would Sandy be thinking if I had done this, what would my brothers and sisters think and say, what about my mates, what about the people I sailed with, and what about the my closest of mates, my Vietnam mates, what would they think?

As I watched that yacht head north, rushing back to the forefront of my mind's eye, to the movie theatre in my mind, it was almost as if I was back on *Kickatinalong*.

I was back sailing down the path of the moon surrounded by the billions of stars of the Milky Way, with that carpet of phosphorescence sliding down the deck as the bow dipped into a wave and scooped it up. The tweet of the dolphins as they sped like bright green torpedoes beside the boat, some of them surfing our bow wave.

There would be no more of this, no more offshore races, no more Sydney–Hobarts, no more sailing in a fleet of 150 yachts on Sydney Harbour, no more boat deliveries, being alive but at inner peace. No more spectacular sunsets, no more lightning shows across the harbour, no more spectacular storms, no matter where they might be, and what about Antigua race week?

Just a sea of nothingness forever.

29th May, 2008, Parliament House Canberra, the day the Australian Government formally recognized the existence of the 2nd D&E Platoon in Vietnam during May and mid-June, 1969. It was exactly 39 years to the day of the battle at Thua Tich where the 2nd D&E Platoon, with 2 Troop, B Squadron of the 3rd Cavalry Regiment ambushed a force, estimated from confirmed intelligence reports, of 700 to 800 NVA and Viet Cong. From the left, Brigadier Neil Weekes, AM, MC, a Platoon Commander with 3 Platoon, A Company in Vietnam with 1 RAR was a mentor to the 4 men of the 2nd D&E Platoon who fought for its recognition. Richard "Barney" Bigwood, Ted Colmer, Don Tate, and Kevin Lloyd-Thomas.

Captain "Gerry" Masson, MID, my maternal grandfather, laying a wreath at a shrine, somewhere in Palestine, to the fallen of Australian forces in Palestine, WW1. P 35

My mother and father on their wedding day, 20th December, 1944. St Georges Cathedral, Jerusalem. It was the same church where Jean's parents were married in 1919.

My father, then Lieutenant, David Lloyd-Thomas, and Mother Jean.

Me as a toddler in the UK, circa 1949.

Having fun on a see-saw.

As an Infantry Instructor, on the steps of the NCO accommodation, E Company, 3rd Training Battalion, Singleton, NSW, 1970.

Taking a resupply break out on operations. L to R: Russ Taylor, Dave Hodgetts and me. Don't know the name of the Armoured Corps soldier in the APC.

Outside the OR's canteen, A Company, 2RAR, Nui Dat.

'Smoko' somewhere in Phuoc Tuy Province. A tired looking soldier.

Smoko and sun tan time at 'The Horseshoe.'

Having a couple of "coldies" between operations. OR's canteen. Bloody well deserved mate.

A trendy looking pipe smoker. You betcha!

About to go on another operation. Nui Dat, Phuoc Tuy Province.

2005 Sydney to Hobart yacht race. "The Weapon" approaching Storm Bay.

2004 Sydney to Hobart yacht race, "Kickatinalong," and that's me sitting on the port gunwale.

I'm the bow man, Sea Quest, aka "The Weapon," Hamilton Island Race Week.

Anzac Day. Great mates, 1 Platoon. L to R Phill Evenden, Peter "Jock" Kennedy, Laurie Tremenheere, and me. Jock and Laurie were both medics, Laurie taking over from Jock when his National Service duty was over.

Getting the spinnaker pole ready to do a spinnaker launch.

CHAPTER 6

REALIZING MY MISTAKES

CHAPTER 6
– REALIZING MY MISTAKES

I don't know how long I sat in the car going through this in my mind and in my mind's eye.

Every now and then I'd look up to look at that yacht, and as it headed north, it started to dawn on me that it was only money. That's all it is, it's only money and am I really that much of a failure? Or am I a failure at all? Is it just that my superfund went belly up and had to be closed, and it's only money after all?

The more of these questions I asked the more relaxed I became. Have you been somewhere like this before, like in debt before? Yes I have. Is that so bad then? Could I actually manage it?

As I asked and answered the questions, little by little I realized I was starting to think more rationally. Maybe, things weren't so bad after all.

You've got your DVA pension for the rest of your life, and you've got a DVA Gold Card, so your health care is completely covered. Then, as I was thinking more and more rationally, it didn't look so bad. I own the car, and I own everything else. Can I live on my pension and pay all my bills? Yes I can. The only downside is the money I now owe the bank, so what could be the worst-case scenario? If interest rates went through the roof, and I couldn't afford the payments it'd be that I'd have to sell the apartment and pay out the bank.

Could I buy somewhere else and be debt free? Yes, I could.

Chapter 6 – Realizing My Mistakes

I backed the car out onto the fire trail and gingerly picked my way back to the car park. I stopped a minute and looked at that yacht again as it was about to sail out of view.

That boat, and whoever was on it, and where ever it had come from, and wherever they were going, without them knowing it, they had literally saved my life.

If it weren't for that yacht and its crew, with whatever decisions they'd made which put them where they were that day, that hour, and that minute when they hove into view, within a few seconds I would have launched the car over the cliff, and even if I changed my mind a split second later, it would be too late. The car would never stop.

The price I paid

It was almost my sanity. It was almost my life.

As I drove home my mind was racing and I found it difficult to breathe. I was taking little short breaths and every minute I'd exhale loudly and then a sound that was the sort of sound you make involuntarily when instantly faced with a fight or flight decision, something like a big huh that takes your breath away.

Over and over again I was saying to myself, "How did I let myself get so low? How did I let this happen? My godfather what did you almost do? My god how did you let it get to this? Fuck, you almost did yourself in. How the fuck did that happen…? What the fuck possessed you to bloody do that?"… and on and on it went.

For most of the almost two hour drive home this is how I was berating myself.

Then it dawned on me…

…For the previous 48 hours I'd hardly slept. I'd let fear take complete control of me. I had sunk so low that I didn't even question it. I'd just let it happen and it was as if fear had lulled the rest of my brain and my mind to sleep, even though I was awake. I'd been almost like an automaton. Fear had made the decision for me, the decision to turn my life off, and I just went along with it.

Life – how precious it is

I walked into the bedroom and laid down on the bed and felt myself drifting off. I was totally and utterly exhausted. I was drained of every single last drop of energy and all I wanted to do was to sleep. I got up and closed the blinds, crawled under the covers pulling the bedclothes up over my head. Within a fraction of a second I was asleep.

My eyes opened slowly as they adjusted to the light. I looked at my watch and it was just past 9.20 and it had to be morning because the morning light was peering through the extremities of the blinds. My god, I'd slept for over 17 hours!

While the kettle boiled I switched on my mobile phone. There were three messages from Irene. Where was I and why hadn't I called? How am I going to tell her what's happened over the last three days? Or should I tell her at all?

I decided to say nothing for the moment because I didn't want to frighten her, and to see what evolved over the next day or two, so I sent her a text message saying my phone had been playing up and it turned out it needed a new battery. It sounded plausible because I had battery

Chapter 6 – Realizing My Mistakes

problems with previous mobile phones. Maybe this phone was going to have the same problem too.

As I started to mull over in my mind the enormity of what I'd almost done, I knew I had to take stock of where I was and the price I'd almost paid. The price of my life.

This is Irene's take on the situation;

I knew Kevin was at his lowest low, but I refused to bail him out this time. We had a pending court case I had prepared him for with the lawyers help, for over a year. The lawyer had told me not to put him on the stand as he didn't think he was mentally fit to do so, and he suggested I took the stand!

No way was I going to do so. I hadn't got us into this mess, Kevin never listened and went behind my back and did what he wanted with me not knowing the enormity of his stupidity, and now they wanted me to take the stand! NO Way! I knew this was a make or break situation, but Kevin never told me about what he tried to do to himself. I was tired of taking responsibility for him and his actions, especially when I had told him NOT to do it. I was tired of the yelling and the abuse he dished out when scared, and I was tired of him not taking responsibility for his own actions. I was tired of not being heard and having to clean up the mess. I was tired of being the strong one, I was tired of not having my needs met. I wanted my old Kevin back.

As Bob Proctor says, "I am responsible for my life for my feelings and for all the results that I get."

When I was flying high, when I was taking responsibility for my actions, I don't recall having negative thoughts, and if I did I turned the negative into a positive. How do I resolve that? How do I get around that hurdle? Hmmmm, that's a bit of a problem. Hmmmm, how can I sort that one out? Ahhh, that's what I'll do.

In his book, *Decisions, Decisions – How To Make The Right One Every Time* (Global Publishing), my very good friend, Steve Coleman puts it like this: "A right decision is one that the decision maker owns. Decision ownership is when the person (or organization) takes full responsibility for it, and they accept its outcome no matter what."

A "Me too" moment?

Over the next days, maybe a week or two at most, I realized I had to go back in time. I had to go back as far as I could think of, to look for the signs of where things had started to go off the rails. Was it one thing? Was it a combination of things? Was it just me, or was it someone else? Or was it me and the influence of others? Was it just bad luck and bad timing, circumstances beyond my control? Or was it that I had abrogated my responsibility to myself?

Failure? What? I've never heard that word before. How do you spell it?

That's the place I had to go back to. What was it like and can I make it work again? Will it work again? What was it? What is it?

In Chapter 7 I'll step you through what I did to make it start to work again.

The mistakes I made – what were they?

I realized that when I first asked for help I'd let ego take control of my mindset.

Chapter 6 – Realizing My Mistakes

When I reflect back, it was the biggest mistake I made, bar none. When I say it was the biggest mistake bar none, *I mean just exactly that. Bar none.* It's said that we're always wise with hindsight – what is it about us human beings, that we've always got 20:20 hindsight?

Why the hell can't we have 20:20 foresight?

Wouldn't that be nice? A situation where you could foresee the outcome of a decision before you actually finally made it and were committed to it. You can examine the outcome and decide if it's what you want, or maybe what you've visioned in your mind's eye, then say yes, looks pretty good to me, I'll make that decision.

One of Steve Coleman's 'Right Decisions.' One where you take full responsibility for it and accept its outcome no matter what.

Letting ego take control? What do I mean by that?

When I first went to the Vietnam Veterans Association, the first thing they started to talk about was getting a TPI through DVA. No that's not what I'm after, I just need help. I'm not one of those bludgers, I just want some help.

Then the referral to the psychiatrist, and after a few sessions, we'll get you a TPI. Your problems will be over and you'll be fine. No, no, no again. I'm not one of those bludgers, I just need help.

I had a fear of the stigma I thought I would have to face. He's just another one of those bludgers on a TPI. What actually happened was, *I had let the fear of what other people might think of me take control of the way I thought.*

Unwittingly, by doing that, by handing over that control of my fear of what others might think, so not allowing the opportunity for having a plan and methodology to be put in place to help take back control, without knowing it, without even thinking about it, and how possibly could I, *I had set myself on the path to destruction.*

Could this be a "Me too" moment for you?

This is the most serious place so far that I have put that question. If you are saying yes, that's me too, then now you know you've got to go and ask for help. *There is no stigma in asking for help.* It's only a fear we have, a fear of what others might think *and it's only in our minds*. The fear can only manifest itself if we let it.

On the first page of this chapter, you've read about those few days in May, 2011, when I took myself to the brink. I've been there, and can relate to anyone who reads this book who may be somewhere on the same path.

You can get off it, and it's as simple as changing your mind. It's a decision, a decision to own it, and to take full responsibility to make it happen, just as you have many times before, to get those things that you've wanted.

As someone who has gone down the path, and down it almost to oblivion, the best guidance I can possibly give you is to go and seek help and do it anonymously, because today you can.

In the Resources Section at the back of the book is a list of organizations that can help you.

Chapter 6 – Realizing My Mistakes

Nobody needs to know, except those who have a need to know, and you'll know who those people are. If there's one more piece of guidance I can give, it's this:

If you're single and have a partner, if you're a married man or woman, and particularly, if you have children, let them know you're going to ask for help. Not only will this lift a load from your mind, it will definitely lift a load from theirs, and you'll have taken the first step to achieving two things.

The first is you are now in a position to take back control of your life. You will control it, instead of it controlling you. Secondly, you will set yourself, and your family on the path to achieving whatever it is in life that you desire, no matter what that is for you. The first thing you will have is happiness. That, along with health are the two most important places you need to be, and everything else will follow.

The Five-Step Life Plan in Chapter 8, and The Seven Pillars Of Success in Chapter 9 will give you a treasure trove of information. If those chapters are a treasure trove, then the website, www.BeatPostTraumaticStressDisorder.com will give you an almost bottomless gold mine.

A dumb observation, or is it?

Life – We Only Have One Of Them – Life is meant to be one of abundance, of health and happiness, of joy and achievement. By making the decision that 'the now' and the future are in your hands and yours alone, by taking control of your life, and with your Master Plan in place, you can do or be anything you want, no matter what that might be.

Stop right now, put the book down, and think about it… from here on in, what are you going to do about it?

More Mistakes – Bitter Lessons Learned

Much of this is from the perspective of 20:20 hindsight, so through this there could be more "Me too" moments for you.

If there are, from what you read next, then you'll know what you need to do, because it's your mind telling you its decision making time. It's pretty well one of two things. Stay as you are and pay a price, or some consequences, or take the decision to live the life of your dreams.

Your choice. But think about it, it's just like any other decision you've made.

When I first got my DVA pension and gold card, I should have sat down with Sandy and made a plan for the future. We had all the material needed to do this. Cassette tapes, DVDs, and books from some of the greatest self-help experts in the world, but I never thought to use them. Just didn't enter my mind. Anthony Robbins, Robert Kiyosaki, Bob Proctor, Jim Rohn, Zig Ziglar and plenty of others.

When we started to argue about money, I should have been able to see, and to recognize what was going on in my mind. Who was in control? The Kevin on the outside? Or the Kevin on the inside. My mind was taking control of me.

What I should have recognized immediately, was that I should have gone and asked for help for the both of us. There were a number of places we could've gone, and programs we could have taken. But no, didn't enter my mind.

Chapter 6 – Realizing My Mistakes

Again, what about sitting down and making a plan that would make us both happy. Never even thought of that. Just didn't occur to me that there was a problem and we should look for a solution.

When it got to the point where Sandy first told me she was unhappy and didn't know for how much longer she could tolerate the way we were living and what our home life was like, again, I should've recognized that it was me, not her, that had brought this about.

There was obviously a problem, but I just withdrew into my shell, bashed the shit out of myself, but did nothing. It just made the situation worse. I resented her conservatism, and she resented seeing me put money into things which just backfired and cost us thousands of dollars.

We should have sat down and made that plan. You know the one? The one we could both agree to because it could work for the both of us and we'd be happy again

When she told me she thought we should consider a separation for a little bit of time to decide what we wanted our future to be like, I rejected it outright. We didn't need to do that. I'm sure we could find a way around things. But what did I do?

All I did was to look at the negatives, and from my perspective, and in my mind, all the negatives were created by her. All she had to do was to agree with me. All she had to do was to agree to do it my way. Alright, I'll go a little bit her way, liquidate half of the shares in the superfund, borrow against the Balmain property and go buy four townhouses in Singleton Heights instead of six. Now that's pretty fair isn't it?

Then I decided I'd do it on my own. Chapter 4 told the story.

A bitter lesson NOT learned

The bitter lesson *I didn't learn*, was what I was doing to Sandy. We'd been married for 32 years, and been together for 35. So bloody selfish, almost unthinking, almost uncaring, and deep down I knew it. But did I have the guts to admit it? No, I didn't, and what I inflicted on her was unforgivable.

It was the first time in my life that, with 20:20 hindsight, I can say, because it was the Kevin on the inside who was in control of my mind, I almost deliberately hurt someone who I loved and who I knew loved me.

Did I give it any kind of the deep, serious thought that it should have deserved, and weigh up the seriousness of the situation and what could be possible? No I didn't. It was very little thought, and with that, it was me who trashed our marriage.

Medication

In 2007, I made the decision to stop taking Zoloft. I'd told Irene sometime before about what a friend had shown me on the internet about the side-effects of Zoloft, and a number of them applied to me.

It was shortly after that, I also made the decision that I'd never ever take chemically based medications again if it could possibly be avoided. Where ever possible I would only use natural remedies. The only way I'd make an exception would be if a doctor said to me, Kevin, either you take this or you're dead.

December 2007, was also the time I stopped smoking, and it came about very quickly.

Chapter 6 – Realizing My Mistakes

It was one of the best things I ever did. The difference to my health and to my lung capacity is nothing short of amazing. I'm not a wowser. Having been a smoker I know just how difficult it is to give up, having given up twice, before finally having success in beating it altogether.

If you are a smoker, the best advice you could get would be to do whatever it takes to stop. You'll never regret it and it will add years to your life.

Mistake – not listening

It's said the mind is like a magnet. There's one hell of a lot of substance in this. Another saying goes something like, "You are what you think about, and what you think about you become."

In the past, that time where everything just worked for me, and everything about my mindset, how I thought, acted and believed, bore very positive results.

Along with a very positive mindset and positive self-talk, *I was an avid listener*, sought opinions and knowledge from others, then took all of this and made decisions. Then those decisions fell in line with my expectations.

When I thought back to where I used to be, and where I'd ended up in 2011, I realized I didn't listen any more. I didn't listen to my intuition, and I didn't listen to other people either. Not the people I should have listened to.

I was going to pay a heavy price for this sometime later.

Is there a "Me too" here?

Mistake – fixated ideas

Without even realizing it, my thinking had become very much black and white. It was either this way or that way and there were no shades of grey in between.

Where at one time I'd explore new ideas, question the status quo, question what I saw as perhaps being old thinking and old ideas, things like, "We've always done it this way," I'd become fixed in many of my opinions.

Not listening, and this tendency towards fixated ideas, was a dangerous brew. The combination of these two deadly things was going to teach me a very bitter lesson, a bitter lesson that was going to be like déjà vu.

Not once, but twice.

Mistake – misplaced trust

Irene seems to have some kind of a sixth sense about this kind of thing, to suss out people and their characters. Most women have a 'BS radar' built in.

Listen to a woman's intuition. It's a bloody sight more sharply honed than a man's is. I don't know where it comes from, but throughout my life, it's a lesson I've learned. It's most likely because they are the nurturers and the carers. They really are. As men, deep down, we know this.

Chapter 6 – Realizing My Mistakes

Listen intently, ask questions, evaluate answers, no fixed ideas, no black and white, and figure out who you can trust. Truly, truly trust. They've got your back, and with no exceptions, and you know it too. You might be surprised how few there are.

Irene said that the biggest mistake she made was to try to help me to fix my mistakes, as I started to rely on her "fixing my problems", and not take responsibility for my own actions. This kind of co-dependence is very detrimental to any relationship!

What do you think this does to your relationship? Is this what's happening with you too?

Maybe another "Me too" moment for you?

First, it takes away your responsibility for yourself, and the next thing that happens when this occurs is that you become "de masculine" and your partner loses her femininity to you. She becomes your mother and savior.

Can you see how detrimental this can be for any relationship?

I also realized that I was allowing myself to keep on repeating the same mistakes I had made with Sandy in my relationship with Irene. Not until Irene stopped 'helping me' and said, "You are on your own kiddo." It was a very hard time for Irene and me, as I felt she let me down and I blamed her for many, many things I had done.

Blame and co-dependence is a great friend and ally for a PTSD sufferer. Trust me, I became an expert at it.

Another "Me too" moment?

It's only when you make the decision to take total responsibility for yourself, your actions and the ensuing decisions you make, that the healing can start.

Once the healing has started, it's then that you can set in place the goals of where you want to end up in life and plans you need to make in all aspects of your life to achieve those goals.

Now you're turning your life around.

CHAPTER 7

TURNING MY LIFE AROUND

CHAPTER 7
– TURNING MY LIFE AROUND

In the aftermath of May 2011, I had started down the path of going back to my past to try to unlock the time when the world was my oyster, and in what state of mind I had been at that time.

At the beginning of 2012, I realized that where I was, was the sum total of all the decisions I'd made in the past, the actions that I'd taken, and the results that I got from that process. I was at where I was purely because of me, and for no other reason. I had no one to blame but myself, because the decisions I'd taken were mine, and mine alone.

It was me who had let myself go so far down in a spiral of self-pity, of cursing myself as a failure, time after time making stupid decisions, making the same mistakes and getting the same results, that I got to the point where I was so far down that black hole that I was prepared to end it all.

It's said that the definition of stupidity is doing the same thing over and over and over again, and expecting a different result, and that's what I'd been doing.

No more black and white

It took me a while to also realize that, to some extent I'd lost the ability and the inclination to 'think outside the dots,' and I'd become fixed in many of my beliefs, where in the past, in most respects I had an open mind, and was prepared to question what was being said or what I was being told.

Chapter 7 – Turning My Life Around

Could this be part of the change on the path to recognizing that perhaps I had to make, for want of a better term, a 'One Kevin'? instead of there being two of me? Was this possible?

When I reflect back on it, when I was rocking and rolling perhaps there was only 'One Kevin' and 'That Kevin' was creative, imaginative, ambitious, always questioning, enthusiastic, motivated, able to enthuse and motivate others, just got things done.

Would the word 'driven' be one you could use to describe 'That Kevin?' Within me, I knew I was starting to turn the corner to rebuilding my life.

In some respects it was two steps forward, then one step back. It was a case where I still had to work hard on myself and I knew there was a journey in front of me. I knew I had to persevere and to learn more about myself so I can help myself better.

Even though I was in debt, I knew I had to make an investment in myself. I sought out people who I felt could help me get a purpose back into my life. Through Irene having been to one of the seminars, I went to a two day workshop with Stuart Zadel. Stuart's 'Think And Grow Rich' seminars were based on the book of the same name, a book written by Napoleon Hill. It was first published in 1938. It's said to be the world's bestselling wealth creation book.

It was the start of the journey I'm still on, one where I see myself as a work in progress. Through Stuart I met Paul and Mary Blackburn. Paul's seminar and his book, 'Beyond Success', was the catalyst for opening up my mind to who and what we really are as human beings, and our human potential.

That led to meeting Daryl and Andrew Grant at their seminar, 'Our Internet Secrets'. Daryl and Andrew are very successful internet entrepreneurs. Andrew had been a paratrooper in 3 RAR, and it was a chance conversation that brought up the subject of Vietnam. From that it led to me telling Andrew my story. It was Andrew, when I told him what had happened to me and what I'd walked away from, who said to me, "Kevin, you have to tell your story. You have to tell people what you went through and how you turned your life around." It was through Andrew I came to find Darren Stephens and Global Publishing.

What happened next?

I made the decision to make another investment in myself and write this book.

I became a voracious reader, and I almost lived at the local library. I read scores of books, I bought 22 more, I read through dozens and dozens of research papers and reports, I went to scores of websites and some of the information I found blew my mind.

It was through all this reading and research that I came across that quote:

"Your Mind Is Like A Parachute, It Only Works When It's Open."

With PTSD, I found information on more than a dozen other therapies that had, and are being successfully used in the community. Variations on cognitive behavior therapy (CBT), eye movement desensitization and reprocessing (EMDR), equine therapy, a whole raft of them. I've found cutting edge scientific research being done in all aspects of trauma and stress, current thinking versus new thinking, all kinds of parachute thinking.

Chapter 7 – Turning My Life Around

While doing research for this book I've been fortunate to meet and now work with some of the most amazing researchers from around the world – Australia, the US, UK, Canada and even Sweden.

These researchers are working at the cutting edge of scientific research into the brain and the brain/gut/mind axis, as well as PTSD, ongoing trauma and chronic stress. These scientists understand that PTSD is similar to a physical wound with similar affects to TBI. In addition, the impact of diet and nutrition, and it's now scientifically proven impact on brain health and wellbeing, is being researched along with supplementation and the possible role it can play in minimizing the effect of brain trauma in combat soldiers.

A world leading expert on genetics working with a retired US Army Colonel are developing a therapy that has a 100% success rate in the removing all symptoms of PTSD. This is ongoing research and, for example, takes a US special forces soldier, with two tours in Iraq, four in Afghanistan and then going back for a fifth, on 17 different medications, who is a walking time bomb, through a special program that leaves him drug free and PTSD symptom free three months later.

An Australian researcher has been investigating the effect of nutrition on brain health for two decades, recently with a special focus on specific nutrients and chronic stress.

The list of researchers investigating the vulnerable brain is growing. These researchers are focused on maximizing brain health and reducing the effects of trauma with the rapid advances in neuroscience fueling this amazing research.

This research is providing actionable help that can benefit servicemen and women directly.

The Five-Step Life Plan outlined in the next chapter is a blueprint for achieving whatever it is that a person who has been in active service may want out of life. A roadmap and plan in which they determine what needs to be done by themselves, to get where they want to be from where they are now and exactly how to do that within their personal time frame.

It's the same approach through the Seven Pillars Of Success outlined in Chapter 9. Amazing information for those who need a road map out of a dark place, and, as you know, a dark place I've been and found my way out of.

By giving back to the veteran community from my life's experience I'm hoping to serve you and them and help them to make a massive difference in their lives and your life too. Thousands of serving men, women and veterans and their families around the world are experiencing huge challenges that have the potential of being removed. That's the purpose behind this book and what is now my life's work.

www.BeatTraumaticStressDisorder.com will give you access to an incredible volume of information, and the world's leading experts across every aspect of what's contained in this book.

CHAPTER 8

THE FIVE-STEP LIFE PLAN

CHAPTER 8 – THE FIVE-STEP LIFE PLAN

"Begin with the end in mind,"
– Steven Covey
The Seven Habits of Highly Effective People

When you first saw this book, there was something about what you read on the front cover that made you pick it up. Within a few seconds you would have turned it over to look at the back cover to see what it said. There was something about what you saw and read that resonated with you.

You probably read it a second time and something inside your mind said 'Hey, that's me too', and then you made the decision to buy the book. You wanted to know more because you had a connection with what you were reading.

What you read about had some parallels for you, and you were absolutely right. Because it's true for most of us who have served and have seen active service.

It was about getting back on track and taking back control of your life. Something in your mind said there was something about where you are now, where you had been, and what you wanted for the future for you, that said this was just what you had been looking for.

What I'm about to step you through is NOT ROCKET SCIENCE!

Chapter 8 – The Five-Step Life Plan

STEP 1 – WHAT DO I WANT TO DO? WHAT DO I WANT TO BE?

This is the start of your roadmap. *The first step in your plan for the rest of your life.*

From a military perspective, did you ever go out on an operation, an offensive, or a training exercise where there was no objective, no purpose no 'end game?'

One morning your Platoon Commander got you out on parade with all your combat gear on, said "Hey guys, just thought we'd go for a bit of a walk, see what's what." "How many days are we out for skipper?" "Don't know, hadn't thought of that."

Do you know of any navy ships that head out to sea, just because the Captain thought it was a good idea, something to do for the day, maybe a week, maybe more, maybe less. Who knows?

If you're in the Air Force, or were at some time, did you ever come across a Squadron Leader who got all his pilots together, and said "Hey boys and girls. Just thought we'd go for a bit of a fly today."

"Where to and what's the objective?" you ask, and he says, "Don't know, just thought it'd be a good idea."

Did you ever decide to go on a holiday without deciding where you were going? Where did you buy the plane ticket to? Oh, you don't know? How's that? What're you going to do on your holiday?" Don't know." So why are you going on a holiday? Don't know. Hadn't thought about that."

Sounds pretty silly doesn't it? Or is it?

This was another mistake I'd made, and there was a bitter lesson to be learned from it. The mistake I'd made, even though I had all this information sitting around in scores of books, heaps of cassettes tapes, and heaps of DVDs, and the seminars I had attended, and the notebooks I'd filled up, *I had never ever sat down to think through where I was actually headed, where I was actually going in life.*

Then the penny dropped. *The price I paid until I realized and knew I'd truly learned a bitter lesson* is almost beyond being able to have a value attached to it. In terms of relationships, I trashed my marriage of 32 years, and almost trashed the relationship with my partner and girlfriend.

In monetary terms, it's close to $1 million. How fucking stupid can you get?

Remember the parachute? *"Your mind is like a parachute. It only works when it's open."*

Keep it at the forefront of your mind as you start to read what comes next.

Once you've read through it, you'll recognize that it's just EXACTLY what ANYONE who has ever achieved ANYTHING has OBVIOUSLY done, and guess what? There are virtually NO EXCEPTIONS!

And second, read this and digest it, and think about it. Digest and accept it because, whether you like it or not, it's just a plain fact.

Chapter 8 – The Five-Step Life Plan

Research and statistics going back to the early 1900s and up until right now, shows that only 5% of us will achieve what we set out to achieve, and 95% of us won't.

There's no bullshit about it, and what's more, this 5% and 95% relates to some other very important things you should know.

Only 5% of the general population will retire with enough money to live out the rest of their lives in comfort, with financial freedom, and able to leave what they have left to their children and their families. *Financial freedom being a circumstance where, even if you live to be 100 or more, you will have plenty of money to do whatever it is that you like from the time that you retire to the time you pop off the planet.*

That's it, only 5% ever have been financially free, and given the evidence over time, it will only ever be 5%.

The other 95% will retire with anything from having to go straight onto a government pension, or maybe one or two years of being able to live a reasonable quality of life before having to go onto a pension, through to others who will get by for most of the rest of their life, but on a no-frills basis, through to those who will be able to afford the odd trip or two and be reasonably comfortable.

Which bit would I rather be in?

Bet you want to be in the 5% and be happy too, right? I thought so, because most of us do, but only 5% of us will.

This is the key question to unlock the answer to where you end up in life.

Ask yourself: If money was no object and I could have Utopia (whatever that means for you) **what do I want to do or to be?**

Now write that down. Why?

It's because *the 5% of those men and women who achieve their life's goals and aspirations have them written down*.

Apart from that, *the irrefutable evidence* shows that writing things down, then reading them out loud to yourself on a daily basis, has them at the forefront of your conscious mind, then imprints them indelibly into your subconscious mind as you then harness its power for the betterment of your life and the achievement of your goals and aspirations.

This is another lesson I've learned when I reflect back on my life's journey. I've come across more people who poo poo this, than those who acknowledge and accept it.

But when I look at and speak with those whom I am now working with on my next project, a project which is directly connected to this book, and will be available to everyone who reads this book, *every single one of them have written down goals, a written plan, and a specific time for their achievement*.

Every one of these people are multimillionaires. Every one of them have done this on their own. None of them inherited piles of money. They are all just ordinary people who have set out a vision for themselves and made it happen. You will meet them on the website. Just bog ordinary people like you and me who aspire to do and to be something better and to live a life of plenty.

Chapter 8 – The Five-Step Life Plan

Every single one of them provides a service to others, and as a result of this, they have become wealthy in the truest sense of the word. They give, and as a result, they get.

For the moment I'm going to work on the basis that, as a reader you will fall into one of the following three broad groups:

- You are in the military and you want to stay in – you want to make the military your career
- You are in the military and you've made the decision that at some point you will leave the military to pursue another career
- You've been in the military and you've transitioned to a civilian career

Whichever of these applies to you, you made a decision. But if you haven't, then I'm sure you'll accept the proposition that at some time you will make a decision along these lines.

Based on the 13 steps to riches in *Think and Grow Rich*, the first step is 'Desire – The starting point of all achievement.'

As part of the overall Life Plan, write down these three things:

1. What profession, job, business or form of employment, or your own business, will you be in as your main life's work?
2. The year and the age at which you wish to retire
3. The exact amount of money you want to have by that time

It could be something like:

I own my own electrical contracting business.
In 2040, I retire at the age of 50.
By 31 December 2040, I have a net worth of $5 million.

Or it could be:

I am the senior Warrant Officer, Class One in my Corps.
In 2040, I retire at the age of 50.
By 31 December 2040, I have a net worth of $5 million.

Or it could be:

I am a Lieutenant-General.
In 2040 I retire at the age of 50.
By 31 December 2040, I have a net worth of $5 million.

It can be anything you like. You could desire to be, and put your total focus on anything, anything at all, and it doesn't matter what it is. What matters is that you do this right now, and as it is in your mind right now.

The sooner you do this, the better it is for you, because you've now made a decision about the direction in which you are going to take your life.

You've now taken the first step of the Five-Step Life Plan.

It doesn't matter a toss what you want to be, or what you want to do. The **critical thing is, you've now made that decision**.

It doesn't matter if you are in the military and your decision is to stay in the military, or you're in the military and you've made the decision that

Chapter 8 – The Five-Step Life Plan

you're going to leave, or if you haven't made up your mind yet, guess what?

You just did.

If you are out of the military you may have already made a decision like this, but it's highly likely you haven't. By asking yourself this question, the way it is asked, and in the context in which it's asked, you've just clarified your future direction, and you've done this for yourself.

You now know what you want to do, and what you want to be, and how much money you want to have, and by which time you want to have it.

A couple of pages ago I wrote about a mistake I had made by a question I had not asked myself, and the question was the same one that you have just answered.

Prior to May, 2011, ***I had never asked myself the question***, "If money was no object, and I could have Utopia, what do I want to do, or to be?"

But now I do know, and it falls under the 4th of the Seven Pillars of Success which we'll come to after we've detailed the Five-Step Life Plan, the 4th Pillar being Purpose and Passion.

Do I have a vision, a burning desire about what I want to leave as a legacy to the world? Yes I do. Is it written down? Yes it is, and it's described in detail. Do I have written plans and goals for its achievement? Yes I do. Do I have a timescale by which they are to be completed? Yes I do. Do I always make them? No I don't. Sometimes things happen that are beyond your control which necessitate making adjustments.

I am now happy, as *I am at peace with myself, as I accept in my mind*, that *the Kevin on the outside had* **no control** *over the Kevin on the inside,* and our marriage broke up in 2001 because *PTSD was still in control of my life.*

It was in control of my life from the time prior to being pushed out the door at ABC Systems in 1994, until some few months after May 2011 when I drew back from driving over that cliff.

I had let PTSD control my life for over 17 years.

What can also happen, and this has happened to me on a number of occasions – I've found a new piece of information that's relevant to what I'm doing or writing, and its significance is such that I've needed to do some research to confirm my understanding. This has taken time which has meant that I've had to make some adjustments to my timetable for getting things done.

Have I done too much research? No I haven't, but at times it too has played its part in me allowing my time and energy to be distracted.

So, what would you like to be able to say about your life?

"Yes, I achieved what I wanted, and I'm really happy" or "Yes I set out to do this and I got most of the way and I'm happy," or something similar to this.

Or it could be, "Gee, I should've done that," or, "I really should have followed that dream," or, "Damn, I should've done that," "I shouldn't have let myself be talked out of doing that."

So this is the next question…

Chapter 8 – The Five-Step Life Plan

STEP 2 – DO I STAY, OR DO I GO?

This is a "Parachute" moment...your mind must be open.

Okay...so what to do?... In?... or... Out?

The decision to leave the military

First of all, this is a major decision, and one you must think through very clearly, and very carefully. There is no place here for assumptions, gut feel, opinions, half-done research, the uninformed opinions of others, pressure from family and friends and so on.

It will require a lot of homework and well informed decision making.

PLEASE DO NOT TREAT THIS NEXT LITTLE BIT LIGHTLY!

If you are married and have children, even more so, because it isn't just you leaving the military, it's your family too.

Just think about that for a moment. But also think about what I said above, the pressure from family like mums and dads, parents-in-law and the like.

Be careful, because it's imperative that you and your immediate family make decisions that are well informed, well researched, best for you and them, and not, repeat, not for outside family.

Why?

They can have the best of intentions, and it may not be apparent at the time, either to you or to them, but experience shows from research, it's their fear for your future that says you should stay close by to them so they can help you out if this happens.

Use the Resources Section at the back of the book to find the services available to you within the military to help you prepare for the transition into civilian life.

AND ANOTHER THING – You'll need to be aware of this and keep it at the forefront of your mind, your thinking, and your decision making:

The military is a unique community within the wider community.

The civilian world is very, very different, and it is imperative for your future wellbeing, and your family's wellbeing that you prepare yourself for it.

It doesn't have the disciplines, the defined structures, nor the regimentation, nor the certainties, nor your mates, and no one's got your back.

Transitioning from the military community to the civilian community and reintegrating into civilian life does not have to be a problem, *as long as you do your homework and know what to expect*.

Most importantly though, what are you going to do for a living when you get out?

Good question?... What ARE you going to do?

This is one of the toughest questions for those who have been in the

Chapter 8 – The Five-Step Life Plan

combat arms. Like SAS, Commandos, Infantry, Combat Engineers, US Navy Seals and the like.

In doing research into current circumstances and situations, so that what is written here is as up to date as possible and reflects the current picture, it's become most apparent that many serving men and women ***do not realize just what skills they have learned in the military***.

In most cases, as young people in their late teens and early twenties, and in many cases, that they take for granted, skills like personal discipline, leadership, man management, teamwork, decision making and adaptability, many, many military people just don't understand that these skills ***have very real value in the civilian world***.

At a reunion last year, a former colleague of mine was telling me about his nephew, and what he was experiencing. His nephew had recently left the SAS after about 15 years of service, including multiple tours of Afghanistan. He had struggled to find employment, and ended up working on a construction site.

Because of his natural leadership skills and ability, directly as the result of his military training and expertise, his employer quickly identified his value as an employee. He was displaying many of the skills and qualities listed on page 73. He was a natural leader, and had won the trust and respect of all his workmates, and all those people who worked around him.

Then things started to go wrong, not with his work, but what was happening in his mind. Construction sites generate a lot of noise, and it started to get to him. It's a fact that, as soldiers, we are 'conditioned' through our training to confront danger. When we are confronted with a firefight, it's not a question of 'fight or flight,' it's fight.

But what happens when we come back from a war zone? We are not 'unconditioned.'

Is this another "Hands up," or a "That's me too" moment?

You're in a restaurant, just like I was a couple of weeks ago, And, by the way, like me, do you ensure you are seated where you can see the exit, such that you can see all the escape routes? You won't sit where there's a wall right in front of you, will you? Rather, you seat yourself with the wall behind you so you can see everything… just in case? You too? I thought so.

Somebody at another table knocks over a bottle of wine and it smashes on the floor. Your instant and immediate reaction is, most likely, just as mine was, to duck slightly, immediately on guard, and say "What the fuck was that?"

And it was the sudden loud noises of tools like big nail guns and jackhammers, a steel bar being dropped that happened from time to time that was 'getting to him.'

He approached his manager to make him aware that this was happening and that he needed some time off to get help to deal with it. Was this going to be OK? His employer was so impressed with him as a worker, with his work ethic, the relationships he'd built with all the people he worked with, the way he handled himself, his ability to make decisions, his leadership skills and the contribution he made, that of course it was okay.

How it was told to me was something like this: "Take all the time you need, and if that's a month, six months, a year, just take it, and we'll put you on 70% of your salary. We want to do this because we want you

Chapter 8 – The Five-Step Life Plan

back, that's how much we value you."

How's that? Not bad, eh?… that can be you too, valued so much that an employer will do whatever they can to keep you.

That's what your military skills are worth! They have massive value. You are a very saleable and hireable commodity, so never, ever underestimate your value as an employee, or as a human being.

This applies whether you have a recognized trade, and also if you don't. ***It doesn't matter. Truly, it doesn't.***

It does not matter a 'tuppeny toss' what branch of the military, or what Corps you are, or were in, it's having these skills that gives you added value as an employee, or as a potential future employee, over and above what a civilian can bring.

Could this be another "Me too" moment?

That's why this could be the one that tells you it's time to take the first step; that it's now time to seek help.

By doing so at the earliest opportunity, and doing it anonymously, you will always be in control because you will have the tools and techniques that allows this.

By ensuring you are always giving added value, you will be valued in return. Smart employers see their people as their most valuable asset and will look after them in times of need, no matter what their role is in the business.

In doing your research, try to identify if a potential employer has this, or a similar view.

Your immediate future and the happiness for you and your family will rely on you doing your homework, *and doing it thoroughly and well.* Make sure you ask them to help, and make it a team effort. After all, it's all of you together isn't it?

Here's a quick checklist:

- Ask the question, "What support services are available to me within the military to help me get prepared for separation?"
- Make sure you find out just exactly what entitlements you have – *it will be dangerous to assume that the military will automatically tell you*
- Make sure you know where to find these support services, then contact them
- Be sure you know what they will require from you
- List all the skills you see yourself as having
- List all the benefits you can think of that you would bring, and their value
- List all of the types of employment you see yourself being capable of
- If possible, list as many as you can of the names of businesses in those fields of employment
- Can any of your family or civilian friends help you in this regard?

Transition support services will help you with things like:

- Help and advice on writing a resume
- Applying for employment
- Writing cover letters for different types of employment applications

Chapter 8 – The Five-Step Life Plan

- Interview techniques
- How to 'sell yourself'
- Techniques on how to contact businesses that are not advertising an employment opportunity – many business look favorably on people who take the initiative to contact them no matter what
- Dealing with rejection
- And more

To put it bluntly, you're going to be on your own for the first time in maybe a long time, and there will be no backup from the military at all. All you will now have is the Department of Veterans Affairs, VVCS, State RSL branches and organizations like Mates4Mates in Queensland.

In the USA it is the VA.

In the UK you have the Career Transition Partnership. Contact information is in the Resources Section.

In the UK, for any other support as ex forces, you will most likely get better support from organizations like Help4Heroes, and Combat Stress. The website will list even more.

You will also need to ensure you know just exactly how you will get your final severance pay, and your DFRDB.

It is also crucially important that you give a great deal of thought and research into how you will manage your superannuation before you separate. You will have a number of options, and your new employer may also allow you to put your military super into their company scheme, which is most likely run on the company's behalf by a fund manager.

So good luck, *you WILL succeed* when you follow any, or all of the ideas, information, tools, techniques and strategies given to you all through this book.

The decision is to stay in the military, at least for another term, or you've already decided the military is your long term career

The world today, for those who choose to make the military their career, is so radically different since the advent of the personal computer, the mobile phone and the internet.

As it does for those who decide to leave, for those men and women who decide to stay, this technology opens up massive opportunity.

No matter what branch of the military you are in, no matter where you are posted, home or overseas, whether you are married or not, whether you have a trade or you don't, whether you are male or female, it doesn't matter what rank you are, or aspire to be, there is amazing opportunity.

You will be the manager of your own career in the military. Only you will know how far you want to go, and it's your decision, and yours alone.

Opportunity knocks – if you want to take it

So, what is this amazing opportunity? And what's so special about a laptop computer, a mobile phone and the internet? Almost everybody has one or both, and automatic access to the internet. Don't they?

Up until 20 years or so ago, you couldn't do this, and until the last ten, or even five years ago, there was limited opportunity. But not now…?

Chapter 8 – The Five-Step Life Plan

Today, a serving career military man or woman can have their own internet business, or multiple businesses. That's right, MULTIPLE online businesses.

Their families can run them or have their own business, either one or several, it doesn't matter. Even the children can have an internet business!

You can have multiple businesses where you don't need an office, you don't need staff, you don't have to carry stock, *and it doesn't even matter what country you're in*.

This is just an idea, just an idea, and yes, it's meant to be there twice.

Why?

Just think about it. It's about building financial independence and financial freedom. If you did get out, you wouldn't need 'a job' because you might have three or four streams of income.

If you are in for the long term, because you do what you love, and love what you do, who says you have to stick to one pay packet? No one does, so why not have several?

In the Seven Pillars of Success, the 6th Pillar is Business. You can explore it further there, in the Resources Section, and even further on the website.

The key issue here is this:

You don't have to be locked in, and neither does your family.

This is one of those *"Parachute moments."* Just think about it.

In summary here, you've elected to stay in the military and make it your career. From what you've read so far:

- Your mind is like a parachute… it only works when it's open
- If you've said "Me too," to seek help anonymously
- Tell your immediate family and those who you feel have a need to know, or you want them to know
- Work as a team. There's strength in numbers and we all need support at one time or another
- Just do it quietly and privately
- You will all be winners
- Then consider the possibilities

Can you imagine a scene like this:

- You and your family have four internet businesses
- They've become really successful over the last three years
- Between them, they now give your family a monthly income two or three times the size of your military pay packet
- You've just bought a new car, just because you can. It's the latest BMW 428i convertible and it looks stunning
- It doesn't matter what rank you are, but let's say you are a Corporal, and you've done three tours of Afghanistan, right at the sharp end
- You're driving in through the main gate to your unit and your CO drives up behind you
- You both go through and park outside Battalion Headquarters

Just imagine what's going through his mind!

What the?! … Just imagine!

Chapter 8 – The Five-Step Life Plan

STEP 3 – WHAT SKILLS DO I NEED?

You've read Part 6 in Chapter One about how I prepared myself for the civilian world once I'd made the decision that I would not re-enlist for another term in the Army. I was finished with it and I was now preparing to create a new life for myself.

While I was still in, I did that marketing certificate through International Correspondence Schools, studying at night and on weekends to complete it in preparation for March 1972 when I was to take my discharge.

The question I'd had to ask myself is, what skills do I have that are marketable, and guess what? At first pass I couldn't think of anything.

When I first thought about it when I'd made the decision to get out, it didn't occur to me that I did have some skills that could translate into the civilian world. I'd become a good instructor, and I knew I was good, even though I had no formal training.

I could become a teacher of some sort, but teaching what? It wasn't something I pursued specifically, nor necessarily had thought of, but nonetheless it was there.

As a forward scout, did I have to have some kind of communication skills? Yes I did. As a section commander did I have to have communication skills? Yes I did.

What it did relate to was that I now had confidence in speaking in front of groups of people. Next, it gave me good communication skills – skills that I was able to build on from having done two tours in Vietnam, and from the two years at Singleton as an infantry instructor.

It wasn't until I'd left the Army and started selling insurance, then found it was not my cup of tea, that I really started to think about the other skills I had.

Task – *defining and honing your skills*

This step is one of research, education, and implementation.

We all have things that we are naturally good at and can do easily, and conversely, there are skills and abilities required to do our job well, but we have to work on them to become good at them.

Some of us have natural mechanical ability, while some of us struggle with it. Some of us are very comfortable with speaking in front of groups of people, while for some of us, it almost scares us shitless. Some of us find it easy to mix with a group in a room, and others of us find this very difficult.

Some of us find it easy to pick up concepts and ideas, but for others of us, we really struggle with it. We have to go back over it several times to actually 'get it.' Then there are all sorts of shades of grey in between, aren't there?

So, what to do about this?

The first step is to define and identify the areas where you know you need to hone your knowledge and skills. Write them down so you don't

Chapter 8 – The Five-Step Life Plan

forget what they are. As well, you need to be honest with yourself.

Once you've defined those specific areas where you need to do some research, determine where it is you will be able to find the information you seek.

What skills do I need?

Consider this: They could be in parallel, either staying in or getting out.

If you're getting out, the additional skills you can acquire before finishing your term of enlistment could well make you more marketable, so this needs to be a part of your plan.

The key issue here is, wherever possible, to set yourself a course of study, and the discipline to do it, in all those areas you've determined you need to hone your knowledge to maximize your ability to do well. This means sitting exams to get any kind of formal qualification.

You've heard about the 7P's haven't you?

Poor Prior Preparation and Planning Leads To Piss Poor Performance – This is just so true in all areas of life, and in almost every respect.

Getting out

Research, then education, now implementation. But what else is good about this?

By taking action, by doing this, it will signal you are proactive, you have initiative, and you are forward thinking. It will be noticed! Be assured, it will.

Staying in

You are in the military and you want to stay in the military. You've chosen to make this your career.

To achieve the goals you have set yourself in the military, it's now time to think through and to plan the courses and training programs that you will need to have completed to achieve these goals.

They will encompass courses which are pre-requisites for promotion, as well as trade training and courses in the relevant technologies applicable to the Corps, Service, or Branch you are in.

Leadership

Leadership roles go to those who show and demonstrate initiative, those who take action, ask questions. By their very actions they demonstrate they are out of their comfort zone but are willing to take the risk, to take action, to learn, and to lead by example. They are typified by the people who are prepared to go first, to say I'll go first, to swallow their fear and just do it, no matter what.

It's not just completing courses and training programs that will set you apart from your peers. It's how you conduct yourself, how you relate to others. It's how you are seen to demonstrate leadership qualities by how you conduct yourself with others, how you earn the respect and trust of those below you, your peer group, and those above you.

It's about being prepared to do, and doing everything you ask others to do, and without exception. It's by doing even more than you ask of

Chapter 8 – The Five-Step Life Plan

others. Just doing it without any expectation of seeking plaudits or pats on the back. You do it because it's just you, that's the way you are.

It's also about how are you conduct your personal affairs. It's about your ethics, integrity, and character, being honorable and honest. It's about fairness and objectivity.

The men and women who attract the respect and trust of their subordinates, peers, and those senior to them are those that demonstrate these qualities.

But let's not forget we are human too. We've made mistakes, we've made poor decisions, and we've done things or said things we regret. Those kinds of things, when we remember them, or are reminded of them, where we feel bad, we feel embarrassed, we feel remorseful and wish the hell we hadn't done those things or said them.

We feel this in a place I call our 'Sanctum Sanctorum'… The place where only you know the truth. We all have it, and we all know the *real truth* about ourselves. That place where we can't bullshit ourselves, where we can't lie to ourselves. It's the place where, when you recall something you said or did, it makes you wince with embarrassment and regret.

This is also the place where character comes from.

STEP 4 – PLANNING AND GOAL SETTING

Almost without exception, this question of 5% as opposed to 95% of men and women reaching their life goals and objectives, shows the 5% have very specific, very detailed and written plans, goals and objectives, where the vast majority of the 95% do not.

In my case, in the life I lead prior to being unemployed, there were only a handful of times when I sat down and wrote out any kind of personal plan or objective.

Although I had invested money and time in myself for personal development *it had not hit home to me just how important written plans and goals were, and how powerful they are*.

It was not until after I turned away from driving over that cliff, and invested more money and time in myself, and through the path of learning I took, that I learned two crucial things.

The first was discovering *that I have to consider that my mind is like a parachute, that it only works when it's open*.

This is just so crucial. It is what underlines and underpins every step in the journey from the moment and the day, the moment when I turned my car around to where I am now.

Write it down, or better still, print it using your computer, then put it somewhere prominent where you will see it at the earliest opportunity each day.

Chapter 8 – The Five-Step Life Plan

"MY MIND IS LIKE A PARACHUTE. IT ONLY WORKS WHEN IT'S OPEN."

The second was, I realized just how essential it is to have clearly written, plans, goals and objectives.

Why? Because I discovered that 99.9% of those men and women in that 5% of the population who achieve their life goals and objectives, have just that. Clearly written plans, goals, and objectives. And what's more, they constantly and regularly review them.

Why? Because things change. Technology changes, economic circumstance changes, governments change, circumstance beyond our control changes, and guess what? We sometimes change our minds too, don't we?

STEP 5 – SUCCESS IS NOT AN ACCIDENT

When you look at the achievements of the world's most successful people there are a number of things they have in common. The first thing that strikes me about most of them is they have immense vision. There are no boundaries to their imagination.

They have such vivid imaginations, and their visions seemed to be burned into their minds and brains. There is no such thing as can't. It seems not to be in their vocabulary. They don't know of anything that can't be done. There's always a way around whatever it is that may appear to be a stumbling block.

If they find they're not able to figure out what that is, they invariably go and find someone who can.

Sir Richard Branson is an absolute master at this. He realizes it's not possible for him to be all things to any business he has.

When you look at so many other successful people, passion is one good word to describe them. They are passionate about what they do.

From a soldier's perspective I'd suggest we could relate to Sir Richard Branson because of the way he comes across and the amazing adventurous life he's led. The things he's attempted that have been capable of taking his life if it all turned to shit. We can relate to that because we've been in that situation too.

From my experience, one of the things that I now hold to be true, is that when things change, and it's not what you want and diverts you from your path, you then have to change things too.

In the time since I've found my way out of that dark place and with all the research and reading I've done, particularly about true success, setting myself on the path of realizing what is now my purpose and passion in life, and turning it into reality, the key factors in achieving it could be summed up as the following points:

Responsibility – we're each responsible for our own life and where it takes us.

Vision – having a vision and no matter how outrageous and unachievable it may seem at the beginning, other people have had what others might describe as outrageous vision, yet they have achieved it. For instance,

Chapter 8 – The Five-Step Life Plan

the Wright brothers and their first flight. How about Jules Verne when he wrote *20,000 Leagues Under the Sea*. Preposterous the experts said. If nuclear submarines could be manned by robots, instead of men having to be fed so having to come back to port, they could roam the seas for decades.

Writing down your goals – in every study I've ever read of, writing down your goals, and reading them out loud to yourself each day brings them to you.

Meditation for visioning your goals – you see them in your conscious mind's eye, they get indelibly imprinted into your subconscious mind, and it goes on its merry way to bring them to you. The power of the subconscious mind is simply staggering in its ability to bring our dreams and goals to fruition.

Belief – Having an absolutely unshakable belief in yourself and that whatever your goal is, it's achievable.

Persistence – never giving up no matter what. Wanting your goals with such passion that you'll do whatever it takes to achieve them. This must be done with ease and grace.

The world's top athletes, adventurers, entrepreneurs, and the successful people in all fields of endeavor do this.

IT'S ALL ABOUT MINDSET, VISION, VISIONING, AFFIRMATIONS, WRITTEN GOALS, SPEAKING OUT LOUD TO YOURSELF.

Professional athletes – So many of them, as part of their training, vision themselves achieving the pinnacle of whatever sport it is that they're involved in. Skiers, marathon runners, high jumpers, pole vaulters, discus throwers, swimmers, racing drivers and the list goes on.

Look at what is being achieved in other areas of human endeavor.

Single, solo, nonstop, unassisted, circumnavigation of the world by yacht – Jessica Watson, the youngest person ever to do it **and a 16-year-girl to boot!**

How the hell did she achieve that? Vision, goal, plan, then whatever it took to get it done.

That's the essence of persistence, never taking "your eye off the ball," and doing whatever it takes until you achieve what it is that you've set out to achieve.

SUCCESS IS NOT AN ACCIDENT – IT DOESN'T COME TO YOU, YOU GO TO IT!

The Five-Step Life Plan ties in with the next chapter, Chapter 9 – The Seven Pillars Of Success

They are inextricably linked together. Master this combination to live the life of your dreams.

CHAPTER 9

THE SEVEN PILLARS OF SUCCESS

CHAPTER 9
– THE SEVEN PILLARS OF SUCCESS

The Seven Pillars of Success? How on earth did I come up with this?

What the bloody hell is a 'Secret of Success?'

Is this some kind of gibberish? Just a whole lot of hollow mumbo-jumbo?

As I clawed myself back from the black abyss I had been in for so long, and as I reflected back on where I had been in my life *before it was thrown into chaos*, then looked at the recent past, I finally knew what was in front of me, and what I had to do, to get back to where I had been. That there were some fundamental truths that all fell into place, made sense, and were logical.

So what were these so called 'fundamental truths?' The process I took myself through was to tell myself, to virtually, in my mind's eye, step outside my body, and to look down from above, asking the question, "How did I function each day?"

The way I was living my life on a daily basis, the states of mind I was in, the approach I took to things, where was I at in my head on a day-to-day basis? What were my relationships like? How did I actually feel? What was my emotional state like? What did a day look like? What did a week look like?

When I had finally cleared my mind, it was like the penny had finally dropped. Within a couple of hours of thinking it through, there it was. It was literally staring me in the face. When I wrote these truths down, initially, there were 26 of them, but there was no logical sequence. I just wrote them down as they came into my mind.

Chapter 9 – The Seven Pillars Of Success

As I read back through my list, the little man who talked to me inside my head was telling me there were close similarities among some of them, and to reduce the number, so each was quite specific and each could stand alone on its own. There had to be some order and logical connection between the items I had written down. I'm asking myself "What does that mean?" And the little man inside my head told me, "There's a logical sequence to these things, and you can't have one without the other."

So that's when I started to ask myself some questions. What has to come first? What has to be first so that you can have all of the rest, enjoy them and make them work for you?

This took me through a process of asking really tough questions with the objective of consolidation, to arrive at a list of things that could stand on their own, and that's how I cut down 26 of my truths, *to seven key elements* that could encapsulate where I had been in what you could call, my previous life.

The little man in my head was also right about there being a logical sequence. *You can't have one without the other because they are all interrelated.*

By stepping myself through this process I arrived at answering the question, "What has to come first?"

It had to be something which was of such fundamental importance to human and individual survival, and it had to be something where you could ask the question, something like, "If I can't, or don't have this, can I have what follows next without it?"

It was through this process that I identified each of the seven key elements, the sequence that made sense, and could stack up against this kind of questioning.

These are the seven key elements, and the sequence that made sense.

It also answered the question of *"What is the logical sequence?"* You can't you have one without the other because they are all interrelated.

Health
Happiness
Wealth
Purpose and Passion
Spirituality
Business
Finance

It dawned on me that it was a mistake I made at least three times before it hit me in the side of the head like someone had thrown a brick at me. I had never written out a detailed life plan setting out my goals and objectives, a time by which I wanted to have achieved them, and a daily plan which asked the question, *"What am I doing today that will bring me closer to my goals?"*

As I said earlier, when writing about the Five Step Life Plan and why you must have one, here I was, with this vast amount of information and wisdom from some of the smartest and wisest people around, people who are millionaires and billionaires, and I had virtually totally ignored it!

Secondly, from the perspective of my father, and what had happened to him. It's here that it also relates to what happened to my mother after my father's passing.

Then third, to the people who I knew were rich in terms of money, and I knew, were also happy, had great relationships with their wives and children, and looked after their employees. People with ethics, integrity, and character.

Why the third? Because in life, I'd also come across men and women who were rich in money terms, but were definitely not nice people. Ethics, integrity, honesty and character weren't things to be considered

Chapter 9 – The Seven Pillars Of Success

by them in their actions, but, hypercritically, it's what they demanded of others, and bleated loud and long when someone did them in the eye.

Health came first. It had to. It did so because, before the big hit, I was healthy in all aspects of my life. During the work week, I'd get up in the morning, do a meditation, then go to the gym for a workout, a ten minutes spa, shower, then off to the office. A good breakfast, some fruit, then into the day.

The results of my annual checkups told me and my doctor I was physically healthy. In my head, I was happy, relaxed, held no fears or concerns for the future.

From the perspective of my father, he had died at 59 from mesothelioma – asbestos cancer. He was not healthy and had not been for some years. Didn't do any regular exercise, and was overweight. If he had gone to a doctor earlier – in the words of Dame Joyce Dawes, at the time the world's leading expert on asbestos cancer – she could have prolonged his life by two or more years.

Happiness came second. For most of us, happiness is our natural state.

From the perspective of my father, I knew he was not happy. I knew this because my mother was not happy, and as a family we were disjointed. Although I think he mellowed towards the end of his life, it was what had gone before which convinced me, that, as a family, we just existed. Happiness was just a fleeting experience.

From the perspective of the rich people I knew and respected, they were happy because their lives were in balance, and so were those of their families.

Third is wealth. Wealth is not about having a lot of money, although most people see it being one and the same thing. If you are not healthy, it's pretty certain that you're not going to be happy, and it's also going to reflect on your family and loved ones, and those around you. Money is just a means of exchange, and genuine wealth is not about personal possessions and money. Genuine wealth is about being in a state of complete wellbeing.

From the perspective of my father, although he was amassing a lot of money, he was not healthy, he was not happy, and from my mother's perspective, she was a second-class citizen in the relationship. My parents lived in a very smart apartment in the suburb of Toorak, one of the top four or five suburbs in Melbourne, and very close to the city. My father drove the very latest Mercedes-Benz. Outwardly, with all this, some might say they were wealthy, but they did not live in a state of complete wellbeing.

From the perspective of others I knew, knowing them as I did, I could say they did live in a state of wellbeing. They are wealthy.

Next is Purpose and Passion. In the Five-Step Life Plan, to determine what we wanted to do or to be, we asked ourselves the question, *"If I could have Utopia, and money was no object, what would I want to do or to be?"*

After I had stepped back from the black abyss I was about to throw myself into, and asked myself that very same question, and for the first time in my life from a very serious perspective, it dawned on me that I had to find an answer.

On reflection, when I was brutally honest with myself I couldn't say I had a purpose that I was focused on, and a passion to achieve it. It wasn't until I met Daryl and Andrew Grant, and through a chance conversation where I told Andrew a bit about my past, including PTSD, driven by those years of unemployment bringing back all the shit from my two tours of Vietnam, that, for the first time in my life, I now have *a true purpose*, and that purpose is now also *the true passion* I have in life.

One of the outcomes of that purpose and passion in life is this book.

From the perspective of my father, absolutely. He put purpose and

Chapter 9 – The Seven Pillars Of Success

passion into rebuilding his career after being medically discharged from the Australian Army. Did he succeed? Yes he did. In 23 years he took himself from a hospital bed and two near death medical experiences, to owning his own business, Scientific Methods Australia Pty Ltd.

He had been invited to the Board of BHP Limited, and had a string of major international companies as clients. If he hadn't been cut down at 59 years of age by asbestos cancer, there's no doubt in my mind he would have been on the Boards of Directors of many major businesses.

Although our father/son relationship was virtually non-existent, I have the utmost respect for his insight, his capacity for original thought, his ability to think outside the square and the ability to identify and bring out these traits in others. He surrounded himself with very, very successful people, and was very highly regarded in the upper echelon of business circles in Australia.

Fifth is spirituality. By spirituality I don't mean religion, and on its own. Spirituality is a state of mind. It's a state of higher being that we can all aspire to attaining. It's about tapping into the universe, seeing all that's good and ensuring that we use its power for the betterment of ourselves as individuals and for doing good to and for others. Almost like the saying, "Do unto others, as you would have them do unto you."

Business comes sixth. It comes before finance because it relates to what we do for a living and who pays us.

But in today's society and in today's world, it takes on a far more significant role. This is the day of the internet, and computer science has changed the world in regard to business, and business has had to change too.

Today it is a whole different ball game, and when we come to business as the sixth pillar of success you will see precisely why, and it's all good.

From the perspective of my father, who knows how big Scientific

Methods Australia would have become? Who knows how many Company boards my father might have ended up being a part of? He would certainly have been on the board of BHP Ltd, now one of the world's global mining giants.

The seventh pillar is Finance. This pillar is about how we manage our money, how to save, how to invest, how not to have to learn the bitter lessons that I did because of some of those stupid mistakes I made.

I made most of those stupid mistakes when I was on my own, and I can assure you I've had to learn some very bitter lessons. Have they been costly? Absolutely. They've cost me shitloads of money.

Those mistakes are also a part of what sent me down the black spiral. Did I learn from them? Yes I did, but almost too late. I'm still in recovery mode,

By getting this seventh pillar right, you will see how, by managing your finances well, understanding money and how it can be used to create, not just having a lot of money, but having true wealth and success too.

Pillar 1 – Health

Key Areas of Health

- Feed Your Brain and You Feed Your Mind
- The Brain/Mind/Gut Health Axis
- Supplements to Maximize Brain/Mind/Gut Health
- The Exercise You Do

In my discussion with Dame Joyce Dawes during the weekend which

Chapter 9 – The Seven Pillars Of Success

was the last time I saw my father alive, she had commented to me about how he had ignored the messages his body was giving him. As a result of that conversation, I made the immediate decision *that I would never ever, ever, ignore what my body was telling me*. If my intuition told me it was more than a common cold and something I should question, I would immediately go and see my doctor and seek to find out what the problem was, what he thought was the solution to that problem, and if that solution didn't work, what would we do next?

I say 'we,' because we, as individuals, are part of the problem, and a part of the solution. If we do nothing the problem just gets worse, and its solution can become far more complex with the potential for it to become life threatening in some cases. By doing something we become a part of the solution.

We'd all accept the proposition that your General Practitioner cannot be expected to know about every single solitary thing in medicine. They're GPs after all, and not specialists in all aspects of medical science.

My GP in Balmain was no exception. To this day, in my opinion, Jonathan Mak is one of the finest doctors I've ever met. I have the most complete and utmost respect and regard for him, both as a doctor and a truly wonderful human being.

In early spring 2009, I felt a little bit of soreness in my right shoulder. It felt as if it was something like a strained muscle. I'm rubbing my shoulder and wondering if I've pulled the muscle while out sailing. It didn't go away, but I didn't think much more about it.

In six very short weeks, I went from having an ache-like pain in my right shoulder, to almost complete paralysis and excruciating pain from the neck down. The paralysis came on literally overnight.

Around 6.30 am one morning, I woke up needing to go to the toilet and in excruciating pain. Doubled over and hardly able to walk, I hobbled into the bathroom, and had to sit on the toilet because I couldn't stand up to have a leak. When I went to stand up I couldn't. Literally down on my hands and knees on the bathroom floor, I pulled myself up on the bench top of the laundry taking my weight on my elbows, such was the pain through my shoulders, my back and hips with my legs not able to take the weight of my body.

Irene had been staying the night, and hearing me gasping and crying out in pain, she rushed into the bathroom to see what was the matter.

This is how she describes what she heard, then saw – *I sort of woke up when Kevin got out of bed, but didn't see what he looked like as he struggled to the bathroom. It was his agonizing cries of pain and crying out help me, help me, I don't know what's happening to me that told me something was radically wrong and I leaped out of bed and raced into the bathroom. There was Kevin with his head in his hands, propping himself up with his elbows, gasping and heaving as he tried to hold on, and there was a terrible look of fear, almost one of terror on his face and in his eyes, with tears running down his cheeks. What's happening to me, what's happening to me? he was yelling out.*

I was aware of what Kevin had been going through with the pain in his shoulders and hips, the cramps and paralysis in his feet and calves, and that Jonathan was endeavoring to figure out what was happening. I had been in the car with Kevin on two occasions when he was suddenly attacked by the cramps and paralysis in his legs, and had to stop the car.

I took his weight and gently lowered him to the floor, and as I did so, made the decision to get him up to Jonathan's surgery as fast as possible. With quite some difficulty I got him into a pair of trousers and a shirt, and virtually carried him like a sack of potatoes to the car. Kevin was hardly able to help himself such was the paralysis and pain he was in. It's only a three or four minute drive to Jonathan's surgery.

We staggered into Jonathan's surgery. Susan, Jonathan's secretary, with a startled and concerned look on her face, asked "What's wrong, what's wrong?" "Kevin can't walk and he's in excruciating pain" I said as

Chapter 9 – The Seven Pillars Of Success

Susan leapt out of her chair then knocked on Jonathan's door and went straight in. "You've got to look at Kevin, you've got to look at him, he's in real trouble." Jonathan had a patient with him but instantly came out of his office, and I could tell straight away he was very, very concerned at what he saw.

He asked Kevin to describe to him what had happened and how he felt. He immediately checked his pulse, then his heart rate. He said something like "I don't know what this is but it's not life threatening. We need to get him to a hospital as fast as possible." I asked Jonathan which one he thought would be best. RPA (Royal Prince Alfred) would be the best because there will be plenty of doctors there and he needs to go straight to Emergency so they can assess him.

It was about an hour and a half later when I was called in and met Dr Neill McGill, a specialist Rheumatologist who was with Kevin. What do you think it is? I asked. Dr McGill answered something like, "Kevin has an auto immune disease named Polymyalgia Rheumatica. It's caused when the immune system attacks itself."

The end result of this was that this disease had destroyed the rotator cuff in my right shoulder. The left shoulder was nowhere near as badly affected and it healed itself. The rotator cuff is the cartilage between the upper arm and the shoulder joint which prevents bone rubbing on bone. In my case I needed radical surgery to be able to get back the use of my right shoulder.

Again, as I have always done since the death of my father, I asked the question, "If you were going to have this done, who would you go and see?" I was referred to Dr John Trantalis, a surgeon who specialized in elbows and shoulders. His opinion was that I could get back about 75% of my shoulder and arm movement, but he would endeavor to give me as much as possible. The testament to his ability as a surgeon is that I now have, as far as my experience tells me to this day, 100% movement. There was about three to four months in a sling, and being very, very careful, along with months of physiotherapy.

He advised me not to even think of going sailing. To put everything on hold, maximize my physiotherapy to the greatest degree possible, check in with him every three months, then in 12 months' time he would assess my situation again and let me know if I could get back on a boat. I followed his advice to the very letter, and along with his skill as a surgeon, and my commitment to physiotherapy, that's why I got back 100% movement. Fucking awesome! I missed 18 months of sailing, but that was a small price to pay to be able to get back to it, knowing I was back to full fitness.

If there was ever any advice I could give **which is of such strategic importance to your life**, then this is it:

Don't EVER, EVER, EVER ignore what your body is telling you. Go to see your doctor!

One of the greatest gifts you could give to anyone, without having to pay for it, is to give the same advice. It could be you'll need to be pushy with your immediate family, and maybe your extended family, and also with your friends. Tell them a story. Tell them the story below. It may make it easier.

Below is a copy of an email sent to me by my great mate, Barney Bigwood. You'll recall Barney from where I wrote about the 2nd D&E Platoon in Vietnam, and from our fight with successive Australian Governments, Defence, and the bureaucracy for its recognition.

In early March, 2016, it was through a chance phone conversation Barney and I were having, he told me he had been to his GP the previous November, and after being treated for the condition he had attended for, he suggested maybe he should have a digital exam of his prostate as he had not had one for over 12 months. She responded by stating "These days we only rely on the PSA blood tests for prostate cancer," and he didn't need one. She then gave him a pathology request for June 2016, that's right, the following year for fuck's sake!

Chapter 9 – The Seven Pillars Of Success

My comment to Barney went something like this, "That's complete fucking bullshit Barney, if you don't have one, you're fucking around with your own life." I then told him about five of my friends, including my older brother, all of whom, within the previous two years, had blood tests which showed substantial changes to their PSA readings, and without exception, each one of them had to have their prostate removed to avoid cancer.

Bluntly put, I told him this. Go back to your GP as fast as you can and demand a referral to a urologist. When you've got that, contact the urologist and ask to see them immediately. You cannot afford to fuck around and waste time. If something goes wrong, you'll be a dead man walking.

The result was he got the referral. He contacted the urologist whose receptionist arranged an appointment for the following Monday.

The immediate result of the examination was the urologist instantly having Barney admitted to hospital to get a biopsy, that he wanted it tested immediately, and the results to be immediately given to him. Barney was in deep, deep shit. His prostate was about to explode. The urologist needed to know exactly what he was dealing with. The result of that, was Barney being admitted to hospital the following day for his prostate to be removed.

He asked the doctor what would've happened if he had waited until June for a blood test. His answer? Something like, "It would have been too late to do anything to save your life. There'd be nothing I could do for you."

Got your phone message mate, had a radical robotic prostatectomy last Thursday. Also took nerves and lymph nodes. Wearing a catheter until the 6th of April when I see surgeon to have it removed and get pathology results.

Mate you saved my life just as much as if you had dived on a hand grenade for me. If I had waited until June I would be ratshit. Thanks for the push and advice mate. I will keep you informed.

Rick "Barney" Bigwood

If you are a man over 40, get a prostate blood test done every year, and insist on a physical examination at the same time so they can see if there are any changes. If your doctor tells you that you don't need to have a physical examination, **that's complete, absolute and utter bullshit! Get another doctor and real quick.**

If you personally have any doubt about this, get on the internet and find out for yourself. You'll find the advice on the internet is that the blood test alone cannot be trusted. The only way your doctor can be absolutely positive that nothing has changed is to feel the prostate for himself. If it has started to change shape it will be a warning sign that you need to keep a very close eye on it.

Better still, because your GP cannot be expected to be an expert on every element of health, have them give you a referral to a urologist, because they are absolute experts in this field.

Although the last few paragraphs have been about prostate health, the same sentiments apply to women. It's essential that you have absolute trust in your general practitioner. Always ask for referrals to specialists, and ask your practitioner a question like, **"If this were you, who would you go and see?"**

No matter what, you have to live life to the full and to do this, you must look after your health.

When it comes to your health, it's absolutely critical, at the forefront of your mind, you have the parachute.

Chapter 9 – The Seven Pillars Of Success

"YOUR MIND IS LIKE A PARACHUTE, IT ONLY WORKS WHEN IT'S OPEN."

This is the time and place, before we get into the real guts (more of 'guts' in a moment) of good health, to lay the foundation of the how and the why of the way I'm going to put this information in front of you.

For the most part, when we think about our health, we think about what we eat, and what exercise we get. Most of the advertising we see is focused on 'eat my product, drink my product, use my product for your skin, use this to clean your teeth with, why you should go to my gym, and you too will look as good as this stunning looking woman with the hourglass figure, teeth so shiny you could shave in the reflection, skin so healthy the seven dwarfs are about to pop out of it, she never gets sick, never has a runny nose, she never farts and when she does, if she does, it never smells!'

For blokes it's going to be the same thing. 'You'll never go bald, your skin will never go flabby, you will always have a six-pack and the woman in the paragraph above will be forever trying to get in your pants.' Whoops… that should have been the other way around!

The reality is there's far more to it than that. Its complex, depends on our genes, the environment in which we as children, have been brought up in – a good one, a not so good one, or a terrible one. The quality of food that we've been given to eat, the sports we've played, and been encouraged to play, and our parents being interested or not interested, the kind of people who we've been surrounded with, how we've been taught, how to regard ourselves reflecting on our self-confidence, our schooling and the encouragement our parents have given us, and so many other factors.

I'm going to encourage you to always **have an open mind**, but even more importantly, **an inquiring mind** as you read through what's below. If it's an area in which you have a particular interest, or sparks your interest, research it further. By doing this you will see the relationships it has with all other aspects of your health. Refer to the Resources Section for more reading.

It wasn't until I realized I'd allowed myself to blindly accept what others told me, and how bad some of that had been for me, that I realized I had to really seriously explore this whole area because it has absolute direct influence on every other aspect of life.

Feed You Brain And Feed Your Mind

Within this, there are two key areas of our anatomy. One is the brain, and the other is the gut. The brain and the mind go together. What we shove down our gullet in the way of food and liquids, and how our gut reacts to it, and what it does with it, will have a direct influence on the health of our brain, our mind, our body and all our other major organs, *and around and around in circles it goes*.

What we eat will determine the health of our brain. The health of the brain will determine the health of our mind, and the health of our mind and how we use it, will determine the health of the rest of our body, and where we end up in life. *It's that bloody simple.*

The absolute bottom line fact of *what our lifestyle is*, where we will end up, and for how long we will live, *is determined by us and us alone by the choices we make*.

I am where I am today as I write this, almost entirely by the choices I've made, and the decisions I've taken about what I will or won't do, and this goes for every single solitary aspect of my life. Where I am today is the sum total of the decisions I've taken.

Ninety-nine percent of where you are right now, has been driven by the decisions you've taken, and only 1% by factors outside your control.

Chapter 9 – The Seven Pillars Of Success

Like Bob Proctor, and author of *You Were Born Rich*, says, "the truth is ***I am responsible for my life, for my feelings, and for all the results that I get.***"

How bloody true… just think about it!… You are where you are because of you. You did make the decisions, didn't you? Just like me too, and I've made a lot of piss-poor decisions.

The research I've done has thrown up two people who have really impressed me with their knowledge and the passion about their subject. They've both written brilliant books, and I'll quote some information from them because I couldn't possibly know all they know, and put it in such a readable and understandable form.

Food For The Brain

Delia McCabe is an absolute world-leading expert on the human brain and how to keep it healthy so it serves your mind and your body at maximum potential.

Delia has been investigating the effect of nutrition on brain health for two decades, recently with a special focus on specific nutrients and chronic stress. That the list of researchers investigating the vulnerable brain is now growing. These researchers are focused on maximizing brain health and reducing the effects of trauma with the rapid advances in neuroscience fueling this amazing research. This research is providing actionable help that can benefit service men and women directly.

For those of us who are older combat veterans, currently serving men and women with active service, and veterans of recent conflicts who have transitioned out of the military, even more important though, is her expertise and knowledge about trauma and stress and the direct impact it has on the health of our brain and what we must do to re nourish it as quickly as possible after the experience of a traumatic or highly stressful event.

An extension of this also, is brain health for people who are regularly subject to high pressure and stress, what supplements could be considered to be taken to minimize its negative effects, and harm to overall health.

From the research that I've done, and from what I've learned from the latest neuroscience research, there is, and will be a lot more information and discussion about this with world experts like Delia on the website.

The Brain/Mind/Gut Health Axis

Dr Giulia Enders is also an absolute world-leading expert in her field. The field of the gut, and just how critical it is to the health of the rest of the body, and the massive role that it plays, is second only to the brain, and in conjunction with it.

It's said that the gut is the body's second brain.

In Guilia's book, there is a whole chapter devoted to the relationship between the brain and the gut. It describes how the gut influences the brain, and the relationship between irritated bowels, stress and depression.

Within this chapter she writes of "Where the 'self' originates."

"Grumpiness, happiness, insecurity, wellbeing, and worry do not originate in isolation in the mind. We are human beings, with arms and legs, genitals, a heart, lungs, and a gut. Sciences concentration on the brain has long blinded us to the fact that our 'self' is made up of more than just our grey matter. Recent gut research has contributed significantly to a new, cautious questioning of the philosophical proposition, 'I think, therefore I am.' One of the most fascinating parts of the brain that can receive information from the gut is the insular, or insular cortex."

To find out more about this cutting edge research you'll need to buy Giulia's book.

Chapter 9 – The Seven Pillars Of Success

How does your pooing work? You'll find out why this is a very important question. She'll even ask you the question if you're sitting properly. Sitting or shitting you might say? Don't laugh… it's serious business… doing the business I mean… just being polite…

In the books written by each of them, there is just such a massive wealth of information, you have to go and buy these books. Don't just take them out from the library. You have to buy them because you can always refer back to them. They are just full of gems of knowledge and wisdom.

Delia's book is titled *Feed Your Brain: 7 Steps to a Lighter, Brighter You* (Exisle).

So that you know just exactly what you should be eating, it also contains stunning recipes from smoothies to salads, to muffins and cookies, soups and main meals. Just brilliant!

Giulia's book is *Gut: The Inside Story of our Bodies Most Under-Rated Organ* (Scribe).

What more can I say than, "Shit, eh!" There's an old saying that goes, "If you don't eat, you don't shit, and if you don't shit, you die." I don't know who wrote it, but it must have been some smart ass, so to speak, who knew what they were talking about! One of those turds who knew something. Whoops. Damn! Politically incorrect again.

This book is just so crucially important to your knowledge and understanding of what starts to happen inside your body once you swallow some kind of foodstuff, a liquid, or anything else for that matter. As an adult you'll learn what good and bad stuff you've done as a result of what you've had to eat and drink, and its potential effects on your body and health. As a parent you will understand what happens, and the results of what you feed your children, or allow them to eat.

The knowledge you will acquire will blow your socks off!

Doing yourself a big favor!

If you are taking any antidepressant medication, ask yourself, "How long have I been taking this?" Then ask yourself this question, "When it was prescribed, did my doctor explain to me how this medication would work, how it would affect my brain, and what the potential side-effects were?" Next question, and this is from me to you, if your doctor didn't explain any of this to you, did you ever look it up on the internet just so that you knew what that medication was doing to you?

I'm asking you these questions because it's critically important, that if you are on antidepressant medication, and/or any other prescribed medication, that you understand exactly what it is doing to your brain. But please, don't think this is alarmist, because it's not. There is no intention to scare you, or to make any stupid claims. Its purpose is to get you to ask some questions, just so you know what you're dealing with.

If it bothers you when you have done this research or asked these questions, go back and ask your doctor to explain it all to you because it's so important that you do understand, and that your medico understands that you are taking an interest in your own particular set of circumstances, and that ***it is a team effort to get you back on track***, such that you might get to a point where you no longer need this medication, because you have taken back control of your mind, and of your life.

A good medico should have no problem explaining any of this to you. What medicine works for me may not necessarily work for you. What works for you may not necessarily work as well for the next person. We're all different, we all have a different genetic make-up, we all have different backgrounds and have had different life experiences which have shaped us to where we are now.

From the research I've done, all of these things have an impact on what might work for one person, and perhaps not as well for someone else. Another medication may be best for them, while you and your medico, working as a team, are ensuring that you are using medication that works for you.

Chapter 9 – The Seven Pillars Of Success

As a result of an Australian aboriginal healer asking me about the medication I was on, had I asked any questions of my treating psychiatrist, and what research I had done for myself, I realized I hadn't asked any of these questions, and I hadn't done any research for myself. I accepted what my medico was telling me and followed his advice, including the medication he prescribed. When I found out what Zoloft was doing to my brain, I could finally understand what had happened to me.

Categorically and unreservedly, I have the utmost trust and respect for the doctor I was seeing at that time. He was the psychiatrist to whom I was referred by my GP when I finally made the decision that I just had to go and get help after the tennis ball incident at the Mortgage Store.

It was he who finally woke me up to the fact that if I didn't do something to help myself virtually there and then, within six months there was a very significant chance that I would end up in a psychiatric hospital, and where I went from there was a case of 'who knows?' Unbeknown to me at the time, and what seemed utterly preposterous if anyone suggested it, the 'who knows?' was to be the rollercoaster ride I went on for the next 11 years.

Everything started to make sense about my behavior, my ability to think, to make decisions, to manage my life on a day-to-day basis, to look at a situation or circumstance, and make an informed and sensible decision.

The exercise you do

We know far more today about our physiology than ever before, and that's all very well and good. We also know how important exercise is for our wellbeing.

When we were in the military, particularly during our basic training, for the first time for many, we found out just how fit or unfit we were. Even though, in most cases, we were reasonably young, we most likely thought we were reasonably fit, until it came time to do things like obstacle courses, 20-mile route marches with full gear on and the like.

That's when we found how fit, or unfit, we were.

It's also reasonable to have to accept that the food we consume today, and the variety of it that wasn't around in the 60s, 70s, and perhaps into the 80s, has had much to do with the major problem today of obesity, and this has a direct relationship to physical fitness.

It's also a proven fact that the quality of much of the fruit and vegetables available today is not as high in nutritional value as it was in the 1950s and prior. This is because of a combination of genetic modification, pesticides, preservatives and the like.

This is a very good reason why you need to know as much as you can about the brain/mind/gut axis, and the kinds of foods that are most appropriate for brain health, and as much as you can about the gut, how it works and why, and the relationship between this, and the importance of regular physical exercise.

In essence, the quality of food that you eat, the types of food you eat, your new-found knowledge about the brain, gut, mind, and what these elements all need to come together, will have an absolute influence on how the quality of the exercise you do will reflect back on your total body fitness and vice versa.

All of the experts agree that some exercise is better than no exercise, even if that's just a 20-minute walk each day.

Make the decision to review your levels of health and fitness in every area. Ask yourself what changes you have to start to make today in your diet, exercise routines, and health habits, to enjoy superb physical health sometime in the future.

The end result?

When you are truly healthy, both physically and mentally, you **WILL** be happy!

Chapter 9 – The Seven Pillars Of Success

The impact on all other areas of your life will be massive – family, socially, and at work, and in every other respect, and across all of the other Six Pillars of Success too.

Pillar 2 – Happiness

It's been said that "Happiness is a state of mind."

It would also be pretty reasonable to say that happiness is something we all want to have.

If we accept that happiness is a state of mind, and that it's something that we would all aspire to have, a happy life and existence on a daily basis, then what do we have to do to make this happen?

In endeavoring to answer this question for myself, it made sense that I should determine how other people defined and describe happiness, so my first port of call was the dictionary. According to Merriam-Webster's Online Dictionary, this is the definition of happiness:

- A state of wellbeing and contentment
- A pleasurable or satisfying experience

It was suggested to me that I should see if I could find what some of the greatest minds on the planet defined as happiness and this is what I found

- *Happiness is the progressive realization of a worthy ideal, or goal. – Earl Nightingale*
- *Happiness is the spiritual experience of living every minute with love, grace, and gratitude. – Dennis Waitley*

- *Happiness is that state of consciousness which proceeds from the achievement of one's values. – Ayn Rand*
- *Happiness is essentially a state of going somewhere wholeheartedly, one directionally, without regret or reservation. – William H Sheldon*
- *Happiness is not a reward – it is a consequence. Robert Ingersoll*
- *Happiness is something that you are and it comes from the way you think. – Dr Wayne Dyer*
- *Happiness is where what you think, what you say, and what you do are in harmony. – Mahatma Ghandi*
- *Happiness is the meaning and the purpose of life, the whole aim and end of human existence. – Aristotle*

As I've gone through the journey of finding my way out of the other side of the black hole, I realized that happiness was one of the biggest and most important things I was trying to get back into my life.

That evolved into what is now my burning purpose and passion in life – wanting to give back into the military community from my life's experience. What came out of that is the Five-Step Life Plan and the Seven Pillars of Success, as I put myself in the shoes of currently serving men and women.

That begged the question, "What about everyone else?" It occurred to me that I had to try to understand how to shape your life so you are happy. If what I've done, and that's to determine what my purpose and passion in life is, and it's brought happiness for me, could this then work for others?

As I found my way out of that Dark Place, what was I really doing? I was searching for happiness again. Having turned my life around, and as I travel down my new path, I've come to realize that, by having direction and purpose in my life once more, I'm finding happiness again.

When I realized this, it made me think far more seriously about happiness and how everything we do, as we go about living our lives, will determine if we are happy or not.

Chapter 9 – The Seven Pillars Of Success

When I reflected back on my life, I knew for sure, that as a child, for the most part I was unhappy. There were times that I felt happy, but the happy times were far outweighed by the unhappy ones.

When I left school and went to work, my recollection of that too was that I was unhappy most of the time. I can only think that it was because of two things. The first was the atmosphere of home life. Always on guard because of what my father might to do. A family living for most of its time in fear of doing something or saying something that would draw his wrath. The second was that I had no direction, no purpose. I had no idea of what I wanted out of life. It was just 'existence.'

Happiness started to come into my life once I joined the Army.

When I go back in my mind's eye to relive some of the events I can remember, I recall that I felt pretty happy within myself. It was me who controlled my life, and the military discipline and regimented way of life was one I was quite happy with. I felt good about myself and I was starting to believe in myself once more.

Then returning home from my second tour of Vietnam, I was confident, self-assured, had belief and faith in myself, and above all I was indeed happy. Seriously happy because I had nothing to feel unhappy about. My life was under control and I knew where I was headed.

Life has just got better and better and better. My 13 years at Blackwood's was very satisfying and I was very happy because I had done well. The same when I went to White International as the operations manager, and the same again at ABC Systems until the ass fell out of my world.

Our degree of happiness will depend on how we are progressing towards what we want out of life and what we want to do or be by the time we want to, or can retire and enjoy the fruits of our labor.

In the resources section at the back of this book you're going to find reference to books written by some of the greatest minds and highest achieving people in the world on how to create and achieve whatever it is out of life that you want.

What follows is from one of Brian Tracy's books, because I'm not able to think of a better way of putting it and communicating to you *what's at the essence of happiness*.

I'm paraphrasing from the back cover of his book *Goals* I made reference to above, because in his book he has distilled the essence of how anyone can live a completely fulfilled life.

> "In psychology, your level of self-esteem determines your level of happiness. Self-esteem is defined as 'how much you like yourself.' Your self-esteem, in turn, is determined by your self-image. This is the way you see yourself and think about yourself in your day to day interaction with others. Your self-image is shaped by yourself ideal. Your self-ideal is made up of your virtues, values, goals, hopes, dreams, and aspirations.
>
> Here is what psychologists have discovered: The more your behavior in the moment is consistent with what you feel your ideal behavior should be, the more you like and respect yourself and the happier you are."

Pillar 3 – Wealth

Wealth – What is it?

Success – What is it?

Now's the time to relate this to the concept of 'success,' the concept of 'wealth,' and the concept of 'happiness.'

I put it to you that these three concepts are related, they are interrelated, and that we have to reasonably define them.

The majority of people relate the concept of 'successful people' to people in positions of power, influence, control or at the top of their career. We hear people being referred to as a successful businessman, a successful lawyer, a successful doctor, a successful property developer, a successful investor and on it goes.

It implies that you have to be well-educated, have a university degree, be a chief executive, have your own law firm, maybe control a large medical practice, perhaps be the chairman of a big commercial or residential building developer, or something similar.

It implies that you should be seen to have the trappings of so-called success. A smart car, a big house, designer clothes and the like.

But what is success? What is it really? Does it imply that if I'm not the head of a large corporation, or in the public eye, or I'm not well known, that I'm not successful?

I'll take you back to my former father-in-law, Ted Brown. Ted was an electrician with the State Rail Authority in New South Wales until he retired at 65 years of age. He worked shift work all his working life at State Rail.

In my view, Ted was also a successful person. Why is this?

Three or four days before he passed on, he had told me he was happy, and if he had his life to live over again, he would not change anything about it.

Ted was successful because he loved his job. He was successful because he went to work each day a happy person. He was successful because he came home at night happy with his day's work. He was a successful person because he looked forward to the next day. He was a successful person because he was happy with what he did for a living, he was successful because he was happy that he could provide for his wife and two children, he was successful because he was happy with where he lived, he was successful because he enjoyed his life and his wife and family enjoyed their life. He was successful because he was content. He was content because he was happy. He was happy because he was successful, and he was successful because he was happy with his life.

He was also successful because he was in control of his life. He was in control of the family finances because he had a budget and a savings plan. His savings plan allowed for his retirement with the ability to have enough money to live well, to be able to go for holidays and enjoy his retirement with his wife Daisy knowing they were financially independent.

This then relates to the concept of wealth.

What *IS* wealth?

For most people, wealth means money, and lots of it. The more money you have, the wealthier you are. He's wealthy, she's wealthy. "He, she, they, come from a wealthy family."

Chapter 9 – The Seven Pillars Of Success

When we use this kind of terminology, what we may really be saying is they're rich. They have a lot of money, maybe lots and lots of money, the family has lots of money, but are they wealthy?

A definition of wealth

In his book, *Rich Dad, Poor Dad*, Robert Kiyosaki puts it this way: "The definition of wealth is the number of days you can survive without physically working (or anyone in your household physically working) and still maintain your standard of living. For example, if your monthly expenses are $5000, and you have $20,000 dollars in savings, your wealth is approximately four months or 120 days. Wealth is measured in time not dollars."

To really be wealthy, a substantial amount of the research done into this, shows you need to be happy too to be truly wealthy. You need to be successful at what you do, happy with what you do, and have a life plan which encompasses your goals and what you want to achieve in your lifetime.

Being truly wealthy says you have great relationships, most particularly with your family, and your children. You have a great relationship with those who work for and with you, those above you and below you too. You have their trust and respect because you've earned it. You've earned it because you treat them with dignity and respect. You treat them the way you expect to be treated as well, with dignity and respect.

Being rich in dollar terms, doesn't make you wealthy. Being rich can just say you've got a lot of money. But that does not necessarily make you successful, happy, or wealthy. That's why they are interrelated.

In my life so far, with all its ups and downs, I've known people who are very rich.

They've got lots of toys, fast cars, big boats and yachts, big houses and several of them. But they don't have happiness, they don't have true friends, and by that I mean mates, real mates. Unless you've also got a lot of money, they don't want to know you, and they certainly don't want to associate with you. They make that quite clear.

From personal experience, they're the sort of person who has a shipwright do $15,000 worth of work on their boat, then refuse to pay them over some nit-picky piece of work they say they'd specified be done a certain way, which is bullshit and they know it. Then it gets changed to the way they want it, and they still refuse to pay. When the shipwright threatens to sue them, they short pay them by $5,000. "Sue me then," is what they say, and have no compunction about it.

By the same token, I know people who are very wealthy and they have a lot of money, but it's not just the money that makes them wealthy, it's how they handle it and what they do with it that counts. It's how they live their lives, and how they treat others.

They give money, and a lot of it, to directly help other people who would never be able to help themselves. These are the poor and the downtrodden, the simple tribespeople in Africa for example, who have to put up with drought and famine and have no way of making any money because their crops are gone and they are on their own. They are the starving, and they and their children die in alarming numbers because, even some of the aid agencies cannot cope. There just isn't enough money to go around for food and medicines to keep them alive.

I'd have no doubt that everyone who reads this book will have seen news items and film about these poor people and their desperate plight.

There's a big, big difference between some of the rich, and the truly wealthy.

You know who you are

In 2013, one of these kinds of people came into my life. This person, who will remain anonymous because that is their wish, made a gift of making an investment in me that allowed me to travel to the USA and the UK to forge relationships with key people who will enable me to unlock the realization and achieve the goals and results of what is my passion and purpose in life, for the rest of my life.

It's taken until 15 months ago when I made the investment in myself to write this book, for the serious groundwork that's been laid to come to fruition, such that it will happen.

I also know people who I call wealthy who don't have bucket-loads of money. They are wealthy because of the way they run their lives, the relationships they have, the way they conduct themselves, the way they treat others, and how they give away as much money as they can afford to worthwhile causes.

Pillar 4 – Purpose and Passion

With this book comes access to a website. www.BeatPost TraumaticStressDisorder.com. The website, from the outset, and on an ongoing basis, gives, and will continue to give, massive amounts of information about the Seven Pillars Of Success, and how, with a purpose and passion of your own, you can have and live the life of your dreams, whatever that means to you.

And it's not just about money. True success is doing what you love, loving what you're doing, it's your purpose and passion in life and that's what drives you every day to live a truly wealthy life.

Prior to May 2011, the closest thing I had to a passion was sailing. Racing in shore and off shore and crewing on boat deliveries was, and still is, an absolute passion of mine. I just love being out on the water, and doing boat deliveries in particular, is a time when I am at absolute peace within myself. There's just something about being out in the elements, being out in nature, and no matter what the weather, even in the most serious of storms, I still feel at peace with myself because I'm doing something that I love.

Did I have a purpose or passion prior to unemployment? I always gave 150% and complete commitment to my employers and to my work colleagues, and particularly to those who were my direct responsibility.

This was also the case as a private soldier. When it came to being a Section Commander, I put everything into being the best I could be. The men who served with me knew I always had their back and would lay down my life for them.

As a part of my nature, I always trusted people until they showed me they couldn't be trusted. Even so, I would give them the benefit of the doubt until it was blatantly apparent that I could not trust them any longer.

It wasn't until some months after I joined the Army in March 1966, that I started to get a semblance of self-belief, self-confidence, a feeling of self-worth, and the feeling that I had some value to offer.

At that time, did I see myself as having purpose and passion? The short answer is no, but when I reflect back on it, particularly when I was in Vietnam, *somewhere within me, a seed was planted*. It was because I'd now been exposed to life, and it was a far cry from the one I'd been leading just 18 months before.

My service in Vietnam on that first tour turned me into a far different person to the one that existed before the idea of joining the Army entered my head. And I do mean existed, because that's what my life was like.

Was I acquiring *purpose* when I volunteered for a second tour of Vietnam? The answer was yes. The seed was now starting to germinate.

Chapter 9 – The Seven Pillars Of Success

Why was that? Purpose was established in my mind and in my being.

The seed of passion came not long after when I was posted to 1 ARU as an instructor. It was here that I became doubly aware of the responsibility I had for the men that I was training, because it was Vietnam, and this is where the bullshit and playing war games with blanks came to an end. This was the real deal, and it was now life and death.

At 3 TB at Singleton as an Instructor, as time went by, passion as a feeling, and as a driver of action, became something that was a part of me.

It then became a case of both of purpose and passion, one intertwined with the other.

It was when I made the decision to apply to the Officer Cadet School at Portsea, to get commissioned as an officer. It was because I had a purpose and passion. I wanted to make the Army my career, and I wanted to become an officer, because I knew, from the experience that I'd had, that I'd be a bloody good one. Sadly, not to be.

Forging a new direction in life

Purpose and passion drove this too. The Army didn't want me as an officer, so I would drive into a new chapter of my life with this purpose and passion. Selling insurance just didn't do it for me and I knew this within six months.

The opportunity I was given by being one of the people accepted into the first Management Trainee Program at Blackwood's was the catalyst for perhaps the first time I'd really put time, effort and thought into planning my future.

I'd had to make a decision before accepting the traineeship at Blackwood's about where my future direction lay.

Some months previously, I'd applied for a mature-age cadet journalist position at the Australian Broadcasting Commission. I got an acceptance the day before my appointment with Dick Hanlon, the Blackwood's General Manager.

Decision time. I was ambitious, and now very self-confident. I made the decision to Join Blackwood's. I threw myself into my management trainee role with absolute purpose and passion. Nothing was going to stop me from becoming very successful within the company.

Purpose is most often defined as the reason why something is done.

My purpose in writing this book, and telling my life story is to show you, the reader how to take back control of your life, or to retain control over it by implementing the Five-Step Life Plan, and ***doing whatever it takes to realize all of your goals and aspirations***.

Passion can be defined as, for our purposes as, "Far more than just enthusiasm or excitement; Passion is ***ambition that is materialized into action***."

For You

Let purpose and passion be an integral part of what are you now do from here on in.

Apply it as the icing on the cake of your life.

As almost all of the most successful people do, write down all of your goals and ambitions, wherever it is in life that you desire to end up.

Be absolutely outrageous and let your mind and your imagination run wild. Vision everything you desire. Houses, cars, boats, yachts, maybe an airplane, maybe a helicopter, maybe one of each. Where do you want to live and in what sort of house? Five bedrooms, five bathrooms and parking for five cars. What about an apartment in London, one in Antigua, one in Majorca, one in New York, and just for good measure one in the Seychelles.

How much money do you want to have in the bank by the time you want to stop working? But do you want to stop working at all?

Your life's work and the goals you've set yourself may well see you doing what you love so much, and loving what you do so much, that you just continue on doing it for the rest of your life until it ends.

There are many, many people like this all around the world and they just keep going because it's their purpose and passion.

Write out your goals, make the plans that will enable you to achieve them, review them every day, make every day a productive day that takes you closer to achieving your goals. Be totally focused, persevere no matter what, and do whatever it takes.

Do this with purpose and passion and make it the driving force in your life.

Pillar 5 – Spirituality

What was it about finding my way out of the black hole that led me to believe that part of life itself and what makes us who we are is what's in our inner self?

It was about changing some of my attitudes and beliefs connected with the events that had sent me heading towards that black hole. It was about no more black and white thinking, but asking questions. It was about opening up my mind

In mid-2015, Irene and I were going through a pretty rough patch in our relationship. Earlier in the year, when attending a seminar, we'd met Nicholas and Susan de Castella. They run an organization, the Institute of Heart Intelligence, and within that, a four day workshop, 'Passionately Alive.'

It was almost an ultimatum, so we made the decision we had to do it.

The first session was on the evening of the day we arrived. To say that I became uncomfortable when Nicholas described the process he would take us through would be an understatement. Essentially I would have to lay my inner self bare. For me that was going to be a big, big hurdle, and I would be doing this in front of everyone, not just Irene.

I discovered that I didn't feel any self-love any more. I'd shut down on the inside, shutting down my feelings, and had lost connection with myself. I had become my own worst enemy, my harshest critic, and my hardest taskmaster.

By biting the bullet, I rediscovered myself. I was finally able to let go of all the shit and pent up anger. To let go of all that had happened to me, the things I could control, and those that I couldn't. I was finally able to start to love myself again and to know and realize that I truly was a loving, lovable and worthwhile person.

This was a big, big change within me. A huge advance in life, not only for me, but also for our relationship.

It hit me with such clarity that, at long last, the final roadblock had been removed. I no longer hated myself, nor blamed myself.

I was finally, finally free, and that was only two years ago.

Chapter 9 – The Seven Pillars Of Success

I'm putting this here because it made me really examine my inner self. Who was I? What values did I stand for? What kind of person was I deep down in my inner being? What were my true beliefs and how did I really value myself?

I had finally been able to forgive myself and forgiven every single person in my life who I felt had wronged me or had deliberately done me harm.

What I did next was to go to the internet and put in – Definition of Spirituality.

From the front page of Google the one that struck me most was the one from Wikipedia. (Spirituality–Wikipedia, https://en wikipedia.org/wiki/Spirituality)

"Modern spirituality is centred on the 'deepest values and their meanings by which people live.' It embraces the idea of an ultimate or an alleged immaterial reality. It envisions an inner path enabling a person to discover the essence of his/her being."

For some people spirituality relates to organised religion. Religion could be defined as a set of beliefs and practices, compared to the definition of spirituality from Wikipedia.

So, commonly put, you could say spirituality is a state of consciousness. This can exist either within or outside of a religion.

In his book, The 8th Habit, (Free Press), Stephen Covey, in Chapter 4 writes of the four intelligences/capacities of our nature. Mental (IQ) – the mind, Social/Emotional (EQ) – the heart, Physical (PQ) – the body, Spiritual (SQ) – the spirit.

Stephen quotes Danah Zohar and Ian Marshall from their book, SQ: Connecting With Our Spiritual Intelligence - "Unlike IQ which computers have, and EQ which exists in higher mammals, SQ is uniquely human and the most fundamental of the three. It is linked to humanity's need for meaning, an issue very much at the forefront of people's minds....SQ is what we use to develop our longing and capacity for meaning, vision, and value. It allows us to dream and to survive. It underlies the things we believe in and the role our beliefs and values play in the actions we take. It is, in essence, what makes us human."

In my humble opinion, there is a direct relationship between spirituality and how a person conducts themselves in life.

A person of true character, conducts themselves with ethics, integrity, honesty, and treats other people, in every respect, fully, the way they expect to be treated themselves, regardless of religion.

Pillar 6 – Business

One way or another, in today's modern world of technology, the opportunities for business are as broad as your imagination.

Even today, despite the thousands of success stories of men and women, and even young children, who've built online businesses turning over anywhere from $10,000 to $100,000, to hundreds of thousands, and into multimillions, with all of the massive advances in technology, the scientific knowledge that we have that we didn't have even just a decade ago, and in many cases, just days, weeks, and months ago, you still hear the skeptics talking about what can't be done, and the best advice that they could possibly give you is that you shouldn't do it either.

They may be your family, maybe your friends, or maybe, your acquaintances. Be careful who you listen to.

Chapter 9 – The Seven Pillars Of Success

So many people are talking about what can't be done, so they don't do it, so if they're not prepared to do it, and the best advice that they could possibly give you is that you shouldn't do it either.

What's this got to do with business? What's it got to do with you as a serving man or woman? Or what's it got to do with you as an ex-forces person or your family?

It's got everything to do with your current circumstance, because today, with the internet and all the technology that's associated with it, never has there been a greater opportunity, because it doesn't matter where you are placed right now, there are potential business opportunities available to you from multiple sources and directions.

It doesn't matter whether you plan to stay in the military, to get out, or if you are already out, or anywhere in between.

In Step One of the Five-Step Life Plan, you asked yourself question, "If I could have Utopia, and if money was no object, what would I want to do or to be?"

Step Two was to ask yourself the question, "Do I stay or do I go?"

There was also a third element to Step Two, and that was you'd been in the military, had taken your discharge and were now in the civilian world.

In Step Three the question was, "What skills do I have?" Here is what you considered:

What skills do I need?

Consider this: they could be in parallel, either staying in or getting out.

If you're getting out, the additional skills you can acquire before finishing your term of enlistment could well make you more marketable, so this needs to be a part of your plan.

The key issue here is, wherever possible, to set yourself a course of study, and the discipline to do it, in all those areas you've determined you need to hone your knowledge to maximize your ability to do well. This means sitting exams to get any kind of formal qualification.

Getting out

Research, then education, now implementation. But what else is good about this?

By taking action, it will signal you are proactive, you have initiative, and you are forward thinking. It will be noticed! Be assured, it will.

Staying in

You are in the military and you want to stay in the military. You've chosen to make this your career.

Remember this bit?

Can you imagine a scene like this:

- *You and your family have four internet businesses*
- *They've become really successful over the last three years*
- *Between them, they now give your family a monthly income two or three times the size of your military pay packet*
- *You've just bought a new car, just because you can. It's the latest BMW 428i convertible and it looks stunning*
- *It doesn't matter what rank you are, but let's say you are an 'OR' and you've done three tours of Afghanistan, right at the sharp end*
- *You're driving in through the main gate to your unit and your CO drives up behind you*
- *You both go through and park outside Battalion Headquarters*

Just imagine what's going through his mind!

Chapter 9 – The Seven Pillars Of Success

What the?!....Just imagine

Step Four was setting goals and setting up a master plan for their achievement.

Remember the "7 P's." **P**rior **P**reparation and **P**lanning **P**revents **P**iss **P**oor **P**erformance!

Now I'm going to take you 'outside the dots' or 'outside the square,' to get you to think radically, and to contemplate what you could do, not what you can't do.

Remember, "If I could have Utopia, and money was no object, what would I want to do or to be?"

In the age of technology today, *if you plan to stay in the military*, you can have an online business, or you can have multiple online businesses. *If you are planning to leave the military*, you could have an online business, or multiple online businesses. The same applies if you've already transitioned out of the military.

There are a myriad of opportunities and options, and now I'm going to 'whet your appetite.'

With today's technology, you can run an eBay business and you don't have to carry stock. You can have that stock in a fulfilment warehouse anywhere on the planet. Your eBay business could be run from your home, no matter what military base you are stationed at. A customer gives you an order and you have it delivered from a fulfilment warehouse.

You can run an Amazon business and solely target the US, or UK, or European market, or the Australian market, or *all of them*, and do it just the same way. Your product, or product range is stocked at strategic Amazon warehouses and they just do it all for you and send your profits to your nominated bank account.

The topic of 'Business,' from the perspective of being in the military, whether you plan to make it your career, or your plan is to transition out, or you are ex-military is massive, and not possible to cover here.

The website – www.BeatPostTraumaticstressDisorder.com will give you far more information on just what the possibilities are, particularly, based on the skills and experience you have because you are, or have been in the military.

Pillar 7 – Finance

Creating Your Financial Roadmap – The Now & The Future

1. What is your final financial destination, and what do you want to achieve? These are your money-based goals.

They will be: Long term, medium term and short term.

Dreaming is a part of goal setting and is, almost always the most fun, because it doesn't matter if you think it is realistic or not at the outset. Then what you do and how you use the power of your mind will have a significant bearing on its achievement.

Bestselling author and property developer, Chris Christoff, in his book *Goal Setting For People Who Can't Set Goals – Proven Tools And Techniques To Achieve Anything You Want*, points out that, "Dreaming without action is wishful thinking," and attributes this to his father for one, and in other forms, to many other people.

You never know what you will be able to achieve if you don't try. Who knew I'd be the author of this book? When setting financial goals, as

Chapter 9 – The Seven Pillars Of Success

with any goals it's important to be specific, to be clear about what you want and how much it will cost. This will make it easier to work out how long it will take you to reach your goals.

You will need a detailed time and objective driven plan to achieve these goals.

2. What is your starting point?

You need to know your current financial position before you can decide on the steps needed to reach your goals. Let's assume that you are starting from zero, but you could be anywhere from deep in credit card debt to having money in the bank. Everyone's different.

3. Set a time frame for when you would like to achieve your goals

Setting a time for achievement makes a goal real and spurs you to act – a deadline makes it seem urgent that you get started. You will need to make sure that the time frame is realistic. You'll only be fooling yourself and there's no point in planning to do something if, from the very outset it's just not realistically achievable.

4. Write down a detailed action plan of what needs to be done to achieve your goals

As with all action plans, this needs to be broken down into manageable steps that are achievable within the time frame it is set.

This is probably the most important step and the one that will get you the most excited, since you will see your goals change from dreams to things you can achieve. There are two ways of breaking a goal into steps:

You can either set time goals, for example, "By December 31, I have saved $5000." The second is to set out action steps. Open up a savings account and make a regular deposit of a specific amount of money into that account from your salary each fortnight.

Next step – budgeting

It's most important that you're realistic and sensible about having a budget. It's most important to track how much money you've got coming in, and where your money is going so you know just where you stand financially as you go along each week, each month, each year.

Income

How much do you actually get in your pay packet?
Any other regular income?

What do you owe?

Any credit card debt?
How much?
Any other loans?
Home loan or property investment loan?

Savings

Got any savings?
How much?
Any investments like shares or property?
What's the current value?

By doing this step, you'll now know your total income, what your financial commitments are, and what surplus funds you have.

Next step – savings plan and investing for the future

To be disciplined and create the ability to be able to save seriously, you need to work out where you put your money so it accumulates as rapidly as possible.

Chapter 9 – The Seven Pillars Of Success

Bank savings accounts these days pay very little interest, so you to need to seek other ways of getting a bigger return from your savings to make them multiply. To do this you can either do the research yourself or alternatively, find yourself a very good Financial Planner.

When you do this, history shows you need to be a bit careful. Seek out large specialist financial planning organizations, and be aware of, and know precisely what you want to achieve and what your risk profile is.

From that, you will be in the best position to make your investment decision so that you grow your savings as rapidly as possible.

Decision – your primary investment strategy

Within the broad spectrum of 'Finance,' and how you manage and grow your money, it's always:

"Caveat Emptor," "Buyer Beware."

I CANNOT EVER, EVER, EVER EMPHASIZE THIS TOO MUCH!!!

In any of these markets and the myriad official subsets of them, particularly in money, commodities and futures, ***WATCH OUT!***

With computer programming and the Internet, you might ***THINK*** you're trading on the Money Market, but you are not, such is the sophistication of the scams you can get caught with. It's only a computer program, and you're not trading anything. Your money will disappear, if not in minutes, within a few hours, or even in a day or two.

How can I say this? In 2015 I got caught in a scam just like I've described above. I'm now part of an international class action against the organization, so I'm not able to name names. I said I made the same mistake three times – this was the third - $40,000 in less than a month! This scam raked in, in just 18 months, over $US500 million from people around the globe. WATCH OUT!

The four major strategies that most people consider are Property, the Stock Market, Money Market, Commodities Market.

Whichever one you decide is the one that you're most comfortable with, you now have some homework to do.

Property

There are three basic options:

1. Accumulate investment property
2. Buy, then renovate, then sell
3. A combination of both

Whichever you choose you'll need to educate yourself.

The stock market

When you consider the global financial crisis of 2008, you need to accept the idea that the fallout from that crisis still affects the global economy, and the stock market, and all underlying markets, even today.

This is also true of the markets within markets, like the Options Market over underlying shares.

The money market

The same 'Rules' apply here. It can be reasonably simple, but then you can step up to another level, and it can, and does, get very complex and sophisticated.

The commodities market

With the advent of markets for *'Derivatives'* of these, and there are a number of classes of these, so *you need to be doubly careful*.

Chapter 9 – The Seven Pillars Of Success

The most crucial thing you will need to accept is that you will need expert guidance, and you must be prepared to spend the time to educate yourself.

From my own experience, having my own self-managed superfund, having lost $350,000, my unequivocal guidance is to **seek expert guidance**, and determine which part of that market in which you will become an expert.

For the both property and the stock market, the Resources Section will provide you with access to people with unimpeachable expertise. The website will give more.

And Lastly

Have a current valid Will – dumb if you don't

It is of crucial importance that you have a Will, and it's also important that you update it as your circumstance dictates. Why?

Go to the internet and type in this question: if I die without a valid Will, who assumes control over my Estate?

If you don't have a valid Will, then a Government legislated entity will decide what happens to your estate. It's sad but true, but Wills and Estates can cause massive family upheaval. Why would you want to do this?

So that your wishes are met for the distribution of your estate, it will be a wise and valuable investment to engage a professional, and appropriately qualified and registered Estate Planner to give you guidance and advice.

Coral Brian-Wheatley, in her book, *Building Wealth in a Self Managed Super Fund: How I Turned $80,000 into $4 Million, And How You Can Too*, describes multiple strategies you too can implement to emulate the success she has had. Coral was able to reach financial independence at age 29.

All I can say is, given what happened with my own self-managed superfund as you've already read about, if only I had Coral as a mentor and guide.

Graham Bibby is an international author, entrepreneur and a world-renowned stock market investment expert. He has appeared on well over 1,000 occasions being interviewed on the likes of the BBC, Reuters, Bloomberg television, RTHK-Hong Kong and CNBC

Graham's private clients are billionaires and millionaires. In his book, *Master Your Mind, Master Your Money: How To Successfully Invest In Turbulent Times*, Graham will share his Global Investing Secrets with you.

Practical investing advice, empowering you to create your life's destiny.

FINAL WORDS

Final Words

Now that you are at the last part of this book, it's worth looking back a little to be able to go forward, with all of the experiences and information that's in here, and how you can use it to build the life of your dreams.

PTSD is no longer something which holds you back in life. In fact it's something that you can harness to create an even better life for you, and for your family, because you've said to yourself, ***that's me too***. That's the first step in taking back control of your life. You are now in control, and it no longer controls you.

The stigma of PTSD is something that you don't have to deal with any more, because you now know where you can go to receive help and no one needs to know that's what you're doing.

With you and your family, the goals you've set for yourself, the goals you set for yourselves as a family, and the plans you've put in place to get there, you're on the way to achieving whatever it is that you want, and there's nothing to stop you.

You now have the tools, techniques, and strategies to be able to have anything that you want, and that means anything. It's as broad and as wild as you can possibly imagine.

You know it's going to take perseverance and commitment, and you know there will be a few roadblocks along with the way. But that's not a problem anymore, because you know there's always a way around that roadblock, either around it, over it, or under it. There's always a way.

You know now too, that even if you don't see yourself with the symptoms of PTSD, that even decades down the track, a circumstance, or a set of circumstances could still throw a spanner in the works as it did with me. By preparing yourself, following the Five-Step Life Plan, being aware of Pillars 6 and 7 in the Seven Pillars Of Success, and endeavoring to set

Final Words

yourself and your family up with multiple streams of income, you will control circumstance. It won't control you.

If you're still in the military, you now know the skills you've acquired, and you know that they're not just the technical or trade ones. At the lowest rank in any service, you now know you've acquired personal skills that many people in the civilian world take a lot longer to get, if they get them at all. The very nature of the military makes you a great team person, a good communicator, and a good decision maker. You're organized and disciplined. As an NCO, you've got leadership and communication skills, and what about the man management skills you get as a result of this. The same with being an Officer.

You know that, if you decide you're going to leave the military at some time to pursue a civilian career, you have a roadmap, that when followed, will set you up for a smooth transition into the civilian world. You'll know what to expect and you'll be prepared. You'll know that you are a very marketable commodity, and your experience and skills have a real value in the civilian world.

If you're no longer in the military, and are dissatisfied with where you are currently at, you now have a roadmap and a blueprint to change all that. It's just a decision. Decision means Stop. If what you are doing now makes you unhappy and dissatisfied, all you now need to do is to make a decision. Stop what you're doing now once you've asked the question in Step One of the Five Step Life Plan, "If I could have Utopia, and money were no object, what would I want to do or to be," and answered that question, set the goals, make the plans required to achieve the goals, then implement the plan.

Success is not an accident, and you know that, "Success Doesn't Come To you, You Go To It."

The world truly is 'your oyster' when you take all that's in this book and on the website.

ABOUT THE AUTHOR

Kevin Lloyd-Thomas
Author, Military Veteran, Business, and Real Estate Professional

Kevin is an author, military veteran, successful in business areas, including real estate.

His military career began in 1966 when he joined the Australian Army. He was posted to the Infantry Corps, and sent to Vietnam in 1967, two weeks after his 19th birthday, where he served as a forward scout, rifleman, and machine gunner in the 2nd Battalion of the Royal Australian Regiment.

He volunteered for a second tour of duty, serving as a rifleman and forward scout with the 4th Battalion of the Royal Australian Regiment. Kevin then served as a section commander in the 2nd D&E Platoon, a platoon that became quite controversial in its short existence, but even 45 years later, still causes bitter and hostile debate.

After completing his second tour of duty, Kevin served for two years as an infantry instructor with the 3rd Training Battalion.

Prior to leaving the Army, Kevin prepared himself for civilian life. He studied at night to earn his Marketing Certificate and went to work for J Blackwood and Son Ltd as a management trainee. Later he began his career in the computer industry, then after almost three years of soul destroying unemployment, found a career in real estate sales, then as a mortgage broker.

Unsurprisingly, Kevin was diagnosed with chronic Post Traumatic Stress Disorder relating to the time he spent in Vietnam. It took him nearly ten years, but he ultimately took control of his PTSD.

In his spare time, Kevin enjoys sailing, ocean racing, surfing, and scuba diving. His volunteer activities involved working with Sailability, and Sailors With disAbilities.

His professional and social associations include the Royal Australian Regiment Association, Vietnam Veterans Association, Queensland Returned Serviceman's League, Southport Returned Serviceman's League Sub-branch, Combined Services Club Sub-branch, Mates4Mates, the Southport Yacht Club and the Southport Surf Club.

Kevin has travelled and worked throughout Singapore, Hong Kong, the Philippines, Vanuatu, Fiji, Bali, the United Kingdom, the USA, Canada, France, Germany, Switzerland, Austria, the Netherlands, Italy and Sweden.

Kevin Lloyd-Thomas is the author of *Beat PTSD* and lives on the Gold Coast, Queensland, Australia.

RESOURCES

AND FURTHER INFORMATION

RESOURCES AND FURTHER INFORMATION

Where To Go To get Immediate Help And Support:

Go to the website below, on the top Tool Bar is a box, "Immediate Help & Support," click on it, and it will take you to a comprehensive list of 24-hour Help Services across five countries.

Website: www.BeatPostTraumaticStressDisorder.com

As a reader of this book, you also have access to the website. There is a huge amount of additional information across all aspects of what's in the book, and it will be added to on a regular basis.

It will include each step of the Five-Step Life Plan, each of the Seven Pillars of Success, the latest research on PTSD and associated conditions such as depression and stress.

There will be interviews with the world's leading experts and researchers to bring the most up to date information available about alternative therapies and treatments. It will be at the leading edge of current research.

If you wish to discuss a matter that could make a significant contribution to the community of serving men and women, veterans and their families and work together with me, please email me at BeatPTSDNow@gmail.com. It doesn't matter where in the world you are. It could be speaking, joint ventures, research, therapies that are working for veterans, anything that will support and help the military and ex-military community and contribute to living a life that matters.

Resources and Further Information

Listed below are some of the key books used as sources of inspiration and information. There were many, many more books and research papers I delved into, too numerous to list here.

When these open your mind into further reading and research for yourself, go into the resources sections of those books where they have them too. You'll find gold mines of information, knowledge and inspiration.

The three books listed at the bottom of this list are there for a particular reason. In my opinion they are 'must buy' books. Why?... They are only small, they're inexpensive, and you could read each one of them in 30–40 minutes. At the end of that time, you will have received so much brain food, mind food, and inspiration it will blow your socks off!...and you could re-read them once a week to keep you inspired to live a magic life... and you'll love the illustrations – just brilliant.

Aftershock – The Untold Story Of Surviving Peace, Matthew Green, Portobello Books

PTSD Resurrected – A Story Of Hope, Andy and Zoe Cullen, Linky Muller

Enemy – A Daughters Story of How Her Father Brought Home The Vietnam War, Ruth Clare, Penguin Viking

Piece Of Mind – How To Tap The Other 88% Of Your Mind, Sandy MacGregor, CALM Pty Ltd

Think And Grow Rich, Napoleon Hill, The Ralston Society (A Must Have Book!)

Goal Setting – For People Who Can't Set Goals, Chris Christoff, Global Publishing

Maximum Achievement, Brian Tracy, Simon And Schuster

Goals – How To Get Everything You Want – Faster Than You Ever Thought Possible, Brian Tracy, Berret Koehler

Decisions, Decisions – How To Make The Right One Every Time, Steve Coleman, Global Publishing

The Virgin Way – How To Listen, learn and Lead, Sir Richard Branson, Virgin Books (and anything else by Sir Richard)

Awaken The Giant Within – How To Take Control Of Your Mental, Emotional, Physical And Financial Destiny, Anthony Robbins, Simon And Schuster (A Must Have Book, and any other book by Anthony!)

The Motivation Manifesto – 9 Declarations To Claim Your Personal Power, Brendan Burchard, Hay House (A Must Have Book, and anything else by Brendan)

The 7 Habits Of Highly Effective People – Powerful Lessons In Personal Change – Stephen R Covey, Free Press (Must Have Book, and anything else by Stephen)

Rich Dad, Poor Dad – What The Rich Teach Their Kids About Money – That The Poor And Middle Class Do Not, Robert Kiyosaki, TechPress Inc (A Must Have Book, and anything else by Robert)

Feed Your Brain – 7 Steps To A Lighter Brighter You, Delia McCabe, Exisle Publishers (A Must Have Book, particularly for parents)

Gut – The Inside Story Of Our Bodies Under-Rated Organ, Giulia Enders, Scribe

Resources and Further Information

Brain Maker – The Power Of Gut Microbes To Heal And Protect Your Brain – For Life, David Perlmutter, Yellow Kite

The Brain That Changes Itself – Stories of Personal Triumph From The Frontiers Of Brain Science, Norman Doidge, Penguin

The Brain's Way of Healing – Stories Of Remarkable Recoveries And Discoveries, Norman Doidge, Penguin

Thrive – The Third Metric to Redefining Success And Creating A Happier Life – Arianna Huffington, WH Allen

Beyond Success – Why Everything You've Ever Dreamed Of Won't Be Enough, Paul Blackburn, Beyond Success Seminars

The Game of Life And How To Play It, Florence Scovel Shinn, Tarcher Penguin (A Must Have Book)

Waking Up – A Guide To Spirituality Without Religion, Sam Harris, Transworld Books

Soul Shifts – Transformative Wisdom For Creating A Life Of Authentic Awakening, Emotional Freedom, And Practical Spirituality, Barbara De Angelis, Hay House Inc

Living In The Light – Follow Your Inner Guidance to Create a new Life and a New World, Shakti Gawain, New World Library

Creating Calm Amid Chaos – Learn How To Destress Your Life, Marney C Perna, Gold Carat Publishing

Don't Die With Your Music Still In You – My Experience Growing Up With Spiritual Parents, Serena Dyer (Daughter of Dr Wayne W. Dyer), Hay House

The Military Guide To Financial Independence And Retirement, Doug Nordman, Impact Publications

Out Of Uniform – Your Guide To A Successful Military To Civilian Career Transition, Tom Wolfe, Potomac Books

Millionaires And Billionaires – Secrets Revealed, Darren Stephens And Spike Humer, Global Publishing

Master Your Mind, Master Your Money – How To Successfully Invest In Turbulent Times, Graham Bibby, Global Publishing

Building Wealth In A Self Managed Superfund – How I Turned $80,000 Into $4 Million And How You Can Too, Coral Brian-Wheatley, Global Publishing

Our Internet Secrets – How to Find Financial Freedom On The Internet, Darren Stephens, Global Publishing

How To Grow Your Business Faster Than Your Competitor – The Secrets To Freedom And Success In 5 Easy Steps, Sharon Jurd, Global Publishing

The Inconvenient Truth About Business Success – The 7 Reasons Why Most Business Owners Do Not Become Millionaires And The 1 Simple Thing That Can Change That, Ian Marsh, Global Publishing

The Automatic Millionaire – A Powerful One-Step Plan to Live And Finish Rich, David Bach, Broadway Books

Resources and Further Information

The Three Little Books For Weekly Reading

The Big Little Book Of Resilience – How To Bounce Back From Adversity And Lead A Fulfilling Life, Matthew Johnstone, Illustrated by Matthew, Pan Macmillan Australia Pty Ltd

The Alphabet Of The Human Heart – The A To Zen Of Life, James Kerr and Matthew Johnstone, illustrated by Matthew, Pan Macmillan Australia Pty Ltd

Quiet The Mind – An Illustrated Guide On How To Meditate, Matthew Johnstone, Pan Macmillan Australia Pty Ltd

As another resource, Contact Business Coach and entrepreneur Irene at www.irenelidvall.com She will be happy to help you.

www.ingramcontent.com/pod-product-compliance
Lightning Source LLC
Chambersburg PA
CBHW060019100426
42740CB00010B/1535